Pocket Guide to Multimedia

Pocket Guide to Multimedia

Dave D. Peck

Delmar Publishers

an International Thomson Publishing company I(T)P®

Albany • Bonn • Boston • Cincinnati • Detroit • London • Madrid
Melbourne • Mexico City • New York • Pacific Grove • Paris • San Francisco
Singapore • Tokyo • Toronto • Washington

Cover design: John MacDonald

Delmar Staff

Publisher: Alar Elken

Production Manager: Larry Main

Art Director: Nicole Reamer

For more information, contact:

Delmar Publishers
3 Columbia Circle, Box 15015
Albany, New York 12212-5015

International Thomson Editores
Campos Eliseos 385, Piso 7
Col Polanco
11560 Mexico D F Mexico

International Thomson
  Publishing Europe
Berkshire House 168-173
High Holborn
London, WC1V7AA
England

Thomas Nelson Australia
102 Dodds Street
South Melbourne, 3205
Victoria, Australia

Nelson Canada
1120 Birchmount Road
Scarborough, Ontario
Canada M1K5G4

International Thomson
  Publishing Gmbh
Königswinterer Strasse 418
53227 Bonn
Germany

International Thomson
  Publishing Asia
60 Albert Street
#05-10 Albert Complex
Singapore 189969

International Thomson
  Publishing–Japan
Hirakawacho Kyowa Building, 3F
2-2-1 Hirakawacho
Chiyoda-ku, 102 Tokyo
Japan

3 4 5 6 7 8 9 10 XXX 02 01 00

Library of Congress Cataloging-in-Publication Data

Peck, Dave D.

      Pocket Guide to Multimedia/Dave D. Peck.

         p.   cm.

      Includes index.

      ISBN: 0-8273-7383-X

1. Multimedia systems.   I. Title.

QA76.575.P428   1997

006.7–dc21   97-22709

                                   CIP

Contents

Part I • Multimedia Concepts

Part II • Media Preparation

Part III • Producing/Authoring/Presenting

Preface

Multimedia, the most dynamic tool since the introduction of the personal computer, is essential for anyone desiring to communicate by using a variety of media types. The ability to integrate text, graphics, animation, 3-D imagery, sound, and video through a personal computer can dramatically change the way any message is presented. Multimedia is useful for developing presentations, computer based training programs, interactive CD-ROMs, web pages, touch-screen kiosks, and much more. There is a lot to learn in the realm of multimedia design, but, you need not know a lot to get started.

Having an understanding of the computer hardware, software, and external devices that make multimedia work will greatly aid you on your quest to develop your own multimedia presentation or product. The goal of this text is to introduce you to these devices and to demonstrate what you need as you become involved in multimedia development.

This pocket guide is designed to bring the novice multimedia explorer to a quick understanding of what it takes to assemble computer-based multimedia projects. Everyone will approach this field with different areas of interest and with different needs. I sincerely hope that this "introduction" will help you quickly become involved in the multimedia process.

Enjoy!

Dave D. Peck

Acknowledgments

Foremost, I thank my family for their support during the development of this project. You are the best!

Thank you Trish, Chad, Lauren, Chris, and Dria.

I would like to acknowledge the contributions of the following companies and industry professionals:

Multimedia Design Corporation: Tom Wheeler and Greg Sobieski; Adobe Systems, Inc.: Patricia Pane, Therese Bruno, Janice Reese; Macromedia: Suzanne Porta, Jane Chuey, Rachael Schindler; Image Club Graphics: Tammy Wing.

Every author's dream is having a great publisher. The Delmar staff is exceptional! Thanks to: Michelle Cannistracci, Nicole Reamer, Larry Main, John Fisher, David Mosher, and Cara Soika.

About the Author

Dave D. Peck is the president of activeMedia Communications, in Brentwood (Nashville), Tennessee. His company specializes in interactive media design which includes: CD-ROM content development, presentation design, information kiosk design, interactive learning systems and software training. Dave is also the author of *Multimedia: A Hands-On Introduction.*

Dedication

This text is dedicated to my wife Trish. Thank you for your many, many sacrifices and your unwavering support of me, and my vision.

Part I

Multimedia Concepts

Chapter One

Multimedia Overview

This chapter introduces you to the concepts behind multimedia, and clarifies the term multimedia as outlined by this book. You will learn about the background as well as the current state of multimedia computing. Chapter 1 also provides a guide for what you can do with multimedia, how to get involved, and how it can help you support your endeavors.

Multimedia Defined

Let's begin this book in a straightforward manner. Let's define what multimedia is! In our attempt to do so, perhaps we should first consider the following question: What constitutes media? Some examples of media are:

- Animation
- Sound
- Graphics
- Text
- Photography
- Video

If any one of the above constitutes a singular form of media, then what constitutes multimedia?

Multimedia: the combination of two or more media types, to effectively create a sequence of events that will communicate an idea usually with both sound and visual support. Typically, multimedia productions are developed and controlled by computer.

Now that I have defined multimedia, perhaps I should differentiate multimedia from the word media. When you think of media, what is the first thing that comes to mind? If you think media is a magnetic tape or a floppy disk, a videotape or CD-ROM, you are right. If you think of media as a television broadcast, a computer-based production, or an audio/visual presentation, you are right again! To clarify the position of this book, I am talking specifically about electronic, computer-controlled multimedia, using a variety of media elements to produce a visual presentation.

The word multimedia brings many things to mind, such as highly technical presentations, computer-based applications, a slide show, or simply a transparency on an overhead projector with narration provided by the presenter. Any one of these elements is a form of multimedia presentation. Multimedia involves the use of more than one media type to communicate an idea or enhance a message. Today, multimedia typically involves the use of personal computers to create and control these media productions. Since the general perception revolves around this theme, so does the nature of this text.

As a practitioner, trainer, and multimedia consultant, I occasionally produce or participate in multimedia seminars. I remember vividly the first seminar that I produced to evangelize the multimedia process. Because it was a small group I always kept the floor open for discussion. In my mind, and in the organization of the seminar, I planned a comprehensive presentation of the entire process, from multimedia history to software choices, from graphic design to the production of CD-ROMS. To my surprise, I discovered that the attendees all came to the seminar with a different opinion of what multimedia was and what they expected to get from the meeting. As with most scripts and presentation materials, I had to make on-the-fly modifications to my presentation and address the issues at hand. Luckily, the medium itself lent perfectly to that type of impromptu customization.

In the early days of presenting, the presentation relied heavily on skillfully designed support devices, such as drawings, charts, graphics, and actual products. Today, the art of presenting is still the same. However, the method of presenting and the new support products have ushered in a new era of sight and sound that add a variety of stimulus to contemporary presentations.

Figure 1.1
The slide has been around for decades, and will continue to be an important form of presentation.

This brings to mind the perception of multimedia in today's marketplace. Many think of multimedia as a huge conglomerate of high-powered corporations controlling the way information is being sent between earth and a satellite for media broadcasting. Others think of it as an over-used technical word to describe a personal computer or another electronic device sold through a local retail store. When a customer walks into a computer store and sees a computer labeled "multimedia ready" what does that mean? In general, the term "multimedia" is being pasted onto many new products and services. Because there are so many products and services defined as multimedia, no wonder the term is so hard to define.

The History of Multimedia

The previously mentioned definition of multimedia states that it is made up of more than one form of media. When we think about multimedia today, we think it is created from new technology. However, several elements of multimedia have been around for quite some time. One example of an enduring media type is the slide (see Figure 1.1). The slide presentation has been the cornerstone of family, educational, and business presentations for decades. The process of mixing two forms of communication, the slide and the narration from the presenter, constitutes a

Figure 1.2 Multimedia processes come from various combinations of devices.

form of multimedia. This form has been perhaps the most popular formula in the business world for decades. Not only has it been successful, it is still successful.

Some of the technology that affects how slides are made and projected may change, but this tried and true formula will continue to exist for quite a while.

In the 1970s, the slide show format was introduced to the computer. This introduction was not to the PC as you know it today, but rather specialized computers, designed specifically to control slide shows. This technology allowed the computer to control numerous projectors, coordinating them in a manner that produced fast-paced dissolves and effects, creating truly spectacular visual presentations. Totally separate from the visuals was the sound track. The taped soundtrack would contain cues that triggered the slide projector(s) to do what it was programmed to do. These projects were very effective and impressive, but took a highly skilled person or team to organize and develop them.

In the 1980s, personal computers were introduced that allowed graphic elements to be "cut" and "pasted" from one document to another. Since that time, software and hardware developers have been scrambling to integrate various forms of media into the personal computer. This is evident today with the plethora of peripheral devices that can be connected to our computers to increase functioning.

Some external devices that have been introduced allow the computer to communicate beyond itself. For example, when the computer needs more storage space an external drive is added to meet the need. When the computer monitor is too small, larger monitors are attached to enhance viewing. To share information with a large audience, connections to a video projector and external sound amplification sources are available. Figure 1.2 illustrates some external devices.

In the 1990s computer manufacturers made their systems more accessible to third-party developers who were anxious to design and distribute their wares to the marketplace. The result of this "open architecture" approach was an explosion of third-party devices. As far as the birth of computer-controlled multimedia was concerned, the industry rolled to the launching pad during this phase.

The Future of Multimedia

Being on the launching pad means that a lot of work and planning have gone into a product or project. Even though multimedia has been around a while in a variety of formats its impact is just beginning in the arena of computerized development and delivery.

Because a big portion of multimedia activity is channeled through computers, one thing is certain: rapid change. Computer models have a shelf life between three and twelve months. They are often replaced with newer, faster, more powerful units. These new units must contain new features in order for them to sell, and selling is what keeps the manufacturer alive.

Along with the change that happens to the computer itself, the peripheral devices that connect to the computer are also forced to change. You may be seeing a domino effect starting here. As these hardware elements begin to change, software products must also change. An example of this was the introduction of the Power Macintosh in early 1994. These new systems propelled the performance of existing Macintosh models into a new dimension. However, when this new hardware was introduced, existing software

1984–1987

Simple slide shows

Basic interactivity

1988–1992

Faster processors

Sophisticated graphical interface

Interactive environments grow

1993–1998

CD quality sound

3-D animation

Presentation software enhanced

Sophisticated authoring environments

Connection to externals

Cross platform development

Figure 1.3 Computer capabilities are constantly changing. Personal computers have evolved gradually to include multimedia capabilities.

did not run much faster. Therefore, software developers were forced to adjust their applications, to make them compatible with the new products, and to take advantage of the speed from this newer technology.

What does this mean? Hardware, peripherals, software, and other products, will be in a constant state of flux from here to eternity (see Figure 1.3). By the time this book is published and in your hands, the specific hardware and software issues will have changed or be in the process of changing. The best way to handle this is to learn how to investigate what is next in line and learn how to integrate it into your current mode of operation. The challenge for companies in the business of publishing technology-based books and distributing CD-ROM-based media, is to get the information to the marketplace while it is current.

Multimedia Products

Evidence of the popularity of multimedia is the abundance of CD-ROM titles being released by companies such as Microsoft Corporation. Microsoft is a dominant player in the area of multimedia title development. Microsoft offers a variety of multimedia titles including: Encarta Encyclopedia, Bookshelf, Cinemania, Musical Instruments, Art Gallery, Fine Artist, Dinosaurs, and many other titles. CD-ROM or electronic publishing will continue to flourish in the future. Although personal computer sales have traditionally been higher in the work place, the home market currently dominates total PC sales.

Another company involved in paving the multimedia highway is Philips Consumer Electronics. Philips was one of the pioneers in the development of CD-ROM technologies. Around 1992, Philips introduced Compact Disc Interactive (CD-i). This product looked somewhat like a typical audio cd player, but it contained some sophisticated features and it allowed the user to control or interact with the contents of the cd. This was one of the first attempts to gain entry into the home market with a "multimedia" product. The concept and design of the product was good. Many software titles were developed initially with the promise of more in the near future. The initial offering went over only fairly well. The price for a consumer product was initially high, but as with most consumer electronics, within a few months the price began to drop.

Price is not always the selling point for consumer electronics. With products like the CD-i, software availability is critical to its success. Once this type of technology is developed, and proven to be viable and in demand, competitors will emerge to claim their share of the market.

The success of the CD-i player, based on total sales, never did meet original expectations. The product had mass appeal but the software, expandability, and marketing of the device, did not keep it afloat in the consumer market for long. However, CD-i has proven to be an excellent product in the area of interactive training. The CD-i format is good but to be able to take the format and apply it for use in a personal computer, with enhanced capabilities is even better. An example of how CD-ROM technology used through a personal computer is a better solution is as follows: An encyclopedia on a CD-i player would only allow you to view the contents on a television. If you wanted to copy information to use in a report, the format did not allow you to do so. In contrast, an encyclopedia for use on a multimedia personal computer will allow you to use the information in other capacities, such as copying data or pictures into a word processor for embellishment.

Becoming Involved in Multimedia

Becoming involved in multimedia does not require a high level of expertise. Most become involved in this process through the need to present, typically to an audience. In the past, presenting to an audience meant the utilization of slides, charts, marker boards, overhead projectors, and other methods. Today, with most information being created and stored on our personal or business computers, the logical step is to take this existing information and display it directly from the computer.

Taking information on your computer and presenting it to an audience may require additional hardware and software. The information you are presenting does not need to be attractive or colorful to communicate what you are trying to say, but using good design has its obvious advantages.

The occasional user, one who needs to make presentations and wants to take these presentations to a higher level, should not be intimidated. Most of us have a personal computer at our disposal. Most of these systems either have the capability to develop graphics, sound, and other types of media, or can be upgraded to do so. If not, the basic system cost is fairly reasonable. If your goal or job description entails the development and presentation of computer-based information, the basic products are easily accessible, either through purchasing or renting.

Multimedia Presentation Tips

If you have a need to present in front of an audience, here are some helpful tips that could save you some time, energy, and even embarrassment.

Presentation Preparation

If you have prepared a presentation on your computer and plan to present it using another computer, perhaps at a different location or meeting site, be aware of potential problems. It is critical that testing be performed on the exact computer that will be used on presentation day. Here are some items, however, that you could use as a checklist when presenting on another computer system.

- Make sure that the proper software is installed. This includes the version that you used to prepare your presentation.

- Having the proper fonts that are used in your presentation is mandatory. Without matching fonts, your presentation text will not conform to your original design.

- Computer Compatibility: If you designed your presentation on a desktop computer that has a fast Central Processing Unit (CPU) and your final presentation will be on a slower system, you may not achieve the same results during playback for the transitions, animation, movies, and other elements that you are planning on using in the presentation. Presentation design should be done with various systems in mind.

- Sound quality will differ from system to system. It is critical that sound hardware be compatible. Also important is the number of people you are presenting to and the room in which the presentation will take place. If sound output is a critical part of your message, make sure that you have the necessary external sound support in order for the sound to be heard.

- Screen colors will vary from monitor to monitor. Screen colors can also change, often dramatically, when projected via an LCD (liquid crystal display) panel or projector, or other projection devices. The application of color should be given serious consideration in the overall presentation, especially related to the device that will be used to present to the audience.

- Color depth can also be an issue. You may have designed a presentation in the "thousands of colors" mode, and your current settings may be at "256 colors." This can be fixed within the system utilities on your computer.

Expectations

The responsibility of preparing presentations has usually been an in-house procedure with most of the responsibility resting on the presenter. In comparison, the desktop publishing revolution of the mid-eighties ushered in a new level of expectation as to what the typical document looks like today. Now we expect near typeset-quality documents from our desktop printers. Likewise, presentation software and hardware is becoming a must. We are also in an era demanding polished audio/visual presentations. We are accustomed to fast-paced information thrown at us via the television and are becoming used to visually stimulating images and sound from our personal computers. When we attend a lecture or a presentation, we expect some form of visual that will keep us entertained and stimulate our thinking. We are so accustomed to entertaining presentations that old technology just will not suffice.

Time and Resources

Learning about hardware and software for developing media presentations does not necessarily need to be a full-time job. Your requirements will vary based on your direct involvement with a project. If you have the support of an MIS or graphics department, then your main concern may be with content and delivery. If you are dependent on yourself to conceptualize, develop, produce, and present, then be prepared to learn about the selected hardware and software products involved. It is not only important to know how to use the individual products, but also how they interact with each other.

Having access to the proper resources is also a key issue. You may have a computer and presentation software, but do you have a projection device that is compatible with your computer? If you must present to a large audience, what is the best presentation method? Do you connect to a television? Do you use an LCD panel with an overhead projector? Do you rent a video projector? Are you even familiar with these products and options?

There are numerous options and each is designed for a specific purpose. Once you establish what your purpose is, the output device or process will be obvious. It is important to know how these various options work, where you can obtain them, and what product will work best for your particular audience. Usually, these issues are not complex to resolve but all of these issues will require forethought and resourcefulness.

Doing Multimedia

If you are going to be a presenter or multimedia user, then you need to have a strong knowledge of what hardware and software products are going to work for you. Learning a versatile presentation program that can incorporate all of the elements that you will ever use is a wise move. When the need arises to give a presentation, usually the conditions will change form for each. When you have plenty of time to prepare your presentation you can be a bit sloppy initially and still have time to perfect your show prior to the presentation date. However, usually the time is very brief between the notification and the actual presentation.

Therefore, be prepared by knowing your software. Stay ahead of the game. When you have to make the impromptu presentation, your focus should be on the actual presentation content, not software issues. If your choice is to use a computer-based presentation program, such as Microsoft PowerPoint, you can use the predesigned templates that will allow you to quickly enter your data and proceed. If you have used this or a similar software product you will know how to take advantage of the templates, artwork, sound, and other features that these programs have to offer. Remember that these programs are tools and should support the creative processes that go into your presentation, not dominate the process with a hard-to-use interface.

Contemporary multimedia presentations have many useful support products that enhance the visual sophistication of your materials such as LCD panels for projecting computer screens through overhead projectors for big screen viewing, and projectors that provide excellent color and clarity in a large format. Another relatively new concept in presentation support devices are remote-controlled presentation devices. These units function somewhat like the controller of a slide projector. With these units, you can control a computer-based presentation from across the room via the remote control. Because these technologies are closely linked to the computer industry, rapid changes will happen in this arena.

Personal Usage

As a presenter, you want to use all of the presentation elements that will prompt your audience to respond. One of the most important elements in making a presentation

Figure 1.4 This chart is clear and precise. Just as in spoken presentation, points should be focused, clear, and to the point.

that is supported by multimedia processes is to know how to access the key functions of the hardware and software that you will use. There is nothing more uncomfortable than spending hours rehearsing your presentation then forgetting a command or procedure that makes your presentation perform as planned.

The art of professional multimedia presentations involves becoming a master of your craft. You should seriously research the software that will do the job for you and learn it well. As a computer user, you are probably experienced in the operation of at least one word processing program. You know how to use the spell checker, set tabs, find and replace words, and other features. You feel comfortable enough to open the word processing application and begin typing, giving total concentration to what you are typing. The operation of multimedia software should also be second nature, allowing you to concentrate on content, not the technical aspects of presenting. A good feature of current software product offerings is that they are becoming easier to use.

If you are a timid presenter, multimedia presentation elements can be your friend. For those uncomfortable in front of an audience, the perfect ice breaker is a gleaming chart, graphic, video or other media element that will dazzle your audience. Any boring statistic or presentation can really shine by using animation, sound, video, or other media elements.

Making Your Point

When using multimedia elements in a presentation, be sure to use discretion in your timing and implementation. The proper graphic or effect can be dazzling and really emphasize a point if used at just the right time (see Figure 1.4). These graphics should be shown long enough to get your point across but should not be left in front of your audience too long. An effective presentation will allow the effect to enter, make its impact, then move to the next level.

George Lucas, director of the *Star Wars* trilogy, has perfected this art form. Some of his movie making techniques include the integration of huge sets and special effects. These sets can cost millions to develop and, as with the *Star Wars* movies, can successfully create the illusion of being in another time and place. In the past, many Hollywood directors thought that if you built these fantastic sets, they must be used throughout the entire movie. Mr. Lucas sees it quite differently. His philosophy is to build the right prop for the right effect, let it fulfill its purpose, then move on. In all of the *Star Wars* movies, you will see this technique used most effectively. A spacecraft or backdrop may have taken months to build, but may only appear on the screen for a few seconds. As you know, many films are successful due to the fact that the special effects are the stars of the show. The result is a vivid impression on your audience.

On the other hand, most of us have gone to movies that have been just the reverse. Total boredom exists when there is not enough change. Remember that we are a generation that thrives on having ever-changing, colorful images and crisp sounds presented for our entertainment. Keep these principles in mind as you contemplate the preparation and presentation process for any type of media presentation. Keep it moving, colorful, and simple. Practice your presentation and look for ways to communicate your point in a simple and straightforward manner. You may also find it helpful to borrow ideas from proven presentations or presenters.

Promoting Information and Ideas

Usually, if you are giving a presentation, either in person or via other media types, you have a message you want to communicate. Your ability to communicate can either be good or bad. As the saying goes, a picture is worth a thousand words. Therefore, if you integrate photographs, along with sounds, graphics, video, and color into a presentation, your chances of effectively communicating your message will increase. Of course this is based on tasteful selection of the elements used to support your presentation.

Presentation content must be able to grab the attention of an audience. It must be both appealing and inviting. There are many players vying for attention these days. As you promote your business ideas, your product must stand out from the others.

Why You Need Multimedia

What is multimedia good for? Multimedia, like the computer itself, is a tool. This tool will assist in the promotion of ideas, concepts, or services that you may wish to promote. There are no limits as to what it can be used for. Here are a few areas where multimedia processes are beneficial:

- Business
- Marketing
- Education
- Edutainment
- Training

Business

Today, businesses use the computer to process virtually all correspondence and internal data particular to that business. As businesses have the need to communicate with the outside world, multimedia processes offer a wide variety of options. Through the utilization of multimedia processes, typical information that is generated on a computer can be converted to dynamic charts, illustrations, and colorful graphics, therefore moving the preexisting information into a new arena.

By using multimedia processes, business presentation takes on a whole new meaning. Visual impact is enhanced with the addition of these dynamic components.

Marketing

Computer-based multimedia productions can take product marketing to a new level. Multimedia techniques can be used at trade shows, for presentations, or to give new life to older products. Electronic catalogs allow companies to send electronic versions of their catalogs to households via the internet or CD-ROM, increasing exposure of their products and increasing sales by making the shopping process easier.

Marketing new or existing products can be greatly enhanced by using multimedia technologies. Products can be marketed in a manner that will provide more detailed and stimulating information than printed media.

Education and Training

In corporate life, you can expect growth, downsizing, takeovers, and turnovers. The one thing that remains constant is change. In this transitional environment, it is crucial that employees are properly trained and stay up-to-date on changing trends. Today's businesses are dependent on trained personnel to perform highly specialized tasks. This requires continual exposure to new training methods.

Figure 1.5 A sample of educational CD-ROM titles distributed by Sanctuary Woods.

One of the most effective uses of multimedia technologies is the conversion of existing printed information into digital format. An example of this is the information found in printed encyclopedias. As this information transfers from print to digital, the information takes on new life. Information that was once static in nature, can now be seen and heard through multimedia technologies. A perfect example of this is the Microsoft Encarta Encyclopedia.

Distributed on a CD-ROM, Encarta Encyclopedia brings information to life. With the capacity available on CD-ROMS, various types of information can be stored to illustrate a particular subject. Here's an example of what can be stored on a CD-ROM:

- 33,000 articles
- 8,000 pictures
- 325 detailed maps
- Hundreds of tables
- Narrated animation
- Six hours of audio and video

CD-ROMS include all of this with a simple interface that includes easy word searching and linking. As this trend continues, more topics will be developed to cover any subject matter that you wish to pursue.

Edutainment

Exactly what is Edutainment? This hybrid term refers to multimedia titles that are part Educational- (Edu) and part Entertainment- (tainment) oriented. Such types of media are products like *Franklin's Reading World, Bit-Bot's Math Voyage,* and *Travelrama, USA,* from Sanctuary Woods (see Figure 1.5). Distribution companies, like

Educorp® specialize in the distribution of CD-ROM software and offer a vast variety of Edutainment titles.

Computer-Based Training

There is currently a major shift happening in the utilization of computers in the area of training. Computer-based training (CBT) is beginning to gain wider acceptance due to the added advantages of the multimedia components. Companies are discovering that computer-based training allows their employees to learn faster as well as achieve better retention results compared to other training techniques. Curriculum development for in-house training is expensive and takes a long time to produce. With computer-based training, however, the individual can move at his own pace. Another plus in computer-based training is the ability to change lessons or data for certain levels of staff training. Many exercises may contain common elements. These elements may need only slight adjustments in order to create these new levels.

Another benefit of computer-based training is that the content can contain a variety of multimedia elements. As a part of the job training, the worker can perform a simulated job function in order to develop an advanced skill level without having touched the actual unit. The integration of audio and video allows this training technology to be a highly effective medium. These processes are particularly successful in the area of flight and driving simulators.

Unique Applications

They are in shopping malls, grocery stores, pharmacies, just about everywhere! Electronic kiosks are becoming a mainstay in our day-to-day lives. The concept behind these multimedia droids is to communicate a message or gather information without requiring an attendant. The medium is an excellent method to advertise and market products and services. Perhaps you have been in a shopping mall and had surveyors approach you, asking if we have a few minutes to complete a survey about a particular prod-

Figure 1.6 A multimedia kiosk refers to a free-standing unit, usually with a touch-sensitive screen.

uct or service. The kiosk is a tireless worker, always there, giving and taking information on demand.

A kiosk is typically a computer and a touch-sensitive screen that allows the user to evoke a command or response by touching a graphic element on the screen. The hardware configuration can vary for these units (see Figure 1.6). Typically a kiosk is a stand or a booth used for point-of-purchase product sales, information handouts, or directory services.

Sometimes a laserdisc player is used to hold a vast amount of video that can be instantly accessed by the user. All of this is hidden from view in the kiosk cabinet enclosure.

Kiosks are capable of producing and gathering the same type of information that the survey teams are paid to gather yet without the intimidation to the consumer. The kiosk environment allows the customer or consumer to approach the device based on the message that the kiosk is presenting. The consumer can also take his time rather than commit to an individual. Kiosks can contain the following:

1. Display Only: Allows the viewer to look and learn without active participation.

2. Interactive Display: Allows the user to learn interactively. The user pushes a key on a keyboard or touches a button on the monitor to go to another screen or

level to learn more about a product or service. This "interactive" learning is extremely valuable because the user is learning at his own pace. The user could also control other devices such as a printer to print a copy of an on-screen instruction or presentation.

3. Information Gathering: Allows vendor to gather information about services, needs, demographics, or other information.

The use of kiosks will continue to grow due to the relatively low overall cost compared to the cost of a manned unit.

Publishing Multimedia Projects

So far in this chapter, we have covered several areas of multimedia. You are probably beginning to see how the term came into existence. Not only are we using multiple mediums, but we are also using them in many environments and for a variety of applications. Let us take a look at using multimedia technologies in electronic publishing.

Though the term electronic publishing seems new, electronic publishing has actually been around for quite a while. Here is a brief comparison of traditional versus electronic publishing. To publish a printed book involves having the support of a publisher, who will pay for the up-front costs associated with the project. The services that the publisher provides include the design, manufacturing, distribution, and sales associated with the development of the product. With electronic publishing, once you develop the content, you are ready to distribute. If this is true, then what are the distribution options for electronic publishing? Perhaps the most visible electronic publishing vehicles are the Internet and the CD-ROM.

Electronic publishing on the Internet can be done by anyone that has access to a computer, the proper software, and a connection to an Internet provider. A basic form of electronic publishing includes processing a document to a bulletin board. A more advanced technique is to have a page published on the Internet. This is a process that allows constant exposure to your information while on the Internet.

Another popular electronic publishing medium is the CD-ROM. This technology, and the amount of information it is capable of containing, allows a wealth of information to be published and distributed. CD-ROMS can contain just about any type of presentation that is developed on a personal computer. CD-ROMS are capable of playing music, voice, animation, three-dimensional graphics, video, and other elements that make multimedia work. Electronic publishing makes multimedia work because it can successfully incorporate all of the elements that stimulate our thinking, feeling, and understanding or retaining a message that was presented using this technology.

Another trend that is becoming mainstream is multimedia magazines. These interactive CD-ROM magazines contain interactive articles, art, music, and presentations from contributing authors and performers, and often include sample software programs.

In traditional publishing, text, photographs, layout, and design are prepared and formatted, then, sent out for printing and distribution. Obviously, the printing, production, and distribution costs are expensive. Producing a CD-ROM product is somewhat similar. You must prepare your text, graphics, photographs, layouts and design as you do in traditional publishing environments. The exception to traditional publishing is that instead of going to press at a printing plant, your electronic file goes to press at a CD-ROM reproduction facility.

If going the route of CD-ROM production, the initial cost of mastering a CD-ROM is fairly expensive, approximately $1,000. Once the master copy is produced, subsequent copies cost around $1 each, based on volume. Distribution on these CDs could be through the mail at a cost of under $1. Compared to the cost of printing and mailing a printed piece, the CD-ROM can offer cost savings.

When developing for on-line distribution, once the presentation is prepared in electronic format it is ready for broadcast.

Of course, most CD-ROM products also include printed support material as well as colorful designed packaging. For the amount of information as well as the type and quality of information you can distribute on CD-ROM, a new world of information technology awaits us all.

The future of CD-ROM publishing could rely somewhat on the publications of the past. The printed information that has been produced through the years is a vast storehouse waiting to be reborn in the form of a computer-based multimedia production. Nothing reflects this concept better than the move of encyclopedias from print to CD-ROM, and products like *From Alice To Ocean*.

From Alice To Ocean is a book/CD-ROM product that chronicles Robyn Davidson's 1977 journey across the Australian outback. The CD-ROM contains narration from Davidson and outstanding photojournalism from Rick Smolan. Through the vision of Apple Computer and other sources, the product was reborn in the form of a CD-ROM, allowing us to join in the journey.

Look for similar projects to be produced from archived information. This technology will also allow the preservation of older forms of media, ensuring that the information will endure for future generations.

On the Edge of Multimedia's Impact

The creative and practical usage of multimedia development is still in its infancy. Over the next few years, expect an onslaught of multimedia titles for entertainment, instruction, and other areas. Look for innovation, not only in titles, but also in the format in which they will be presented. Probably one feature that will be refined in the next few years is the ability to use the same title on various computer systems. This is more common today due to the corroboration between hardware and software vendors, and the need to distribute information to anyone, no matter which computer he uses.

The industry has come a long way in the past ten years. When considering the current state of hardware and software technology, imagine the state-of-the-art ten years from now!

Chapter Two

Getting Involved

You may be driven to become involved in multimedia as a result of your chosen course of educational studies, your personal interest in the medium, or because you are trying to keep up with the current trends in business communications. One thing is certain, we must stay abreast of the changes in this field.

If you are entering the multimedia arena just to find out what it is about, you will be amazed at what lies ahead. If you are being forced to learn this technology to develop a new set of presentation skills or even to begin developing a multimedia title for distribution, then you obviously have a concept or need that is driving you to become involved. This chapter will help clarify how to "get your feet wet" in the multimedia process.

The Need to Develop

No matter what your reason for joining the multimedia revolution, you will find that it is a fascinating environment, offering new ways to express any message. There is much to learn about the individual mediums and how they work cohesively to form a single product. Once the direction of your product or production is established, you can begin to assemble the pieces.

Acquiring Resources

You may find that entering the world of multimedia is very linear, requiring the mastery of only a couple of exter-

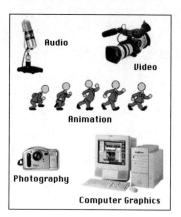

Figure 2.1
Some of the resources involved in the creation of multimedia.

nal sources. This will solely be based on what you are going to do with it. Remember the idea that a simple slide show is a form of multimedia. On the other hand, your intentions for a multimedia production may require many resources and external devices to properly produce your product.

Each project or product that you develop will have its own process development path to follow during the preparation stages. The inter-working of all of these processes is fairly straightforward. For example, if you want to include a photograph in your production then you only have a few options to get this information into your computer. These options include: scanning, digital camera input, video camera image capture, or acquiring an image through a clip-photography resource.

Acquiring various resources requires knowledge of incorporating the various images, sound, and video files into your computer to create a cohesive production. Through the study and observation of the products and processes, the pieces should fit together easily.

If you are a novice to computing or multimedia production, consult with instructors, practitioners, or computer professionals that have expertise in this area. Find out what your limitations are in the realm of acquiring the numerous components that constitute a multimedia production. Your presentation may vary from others. Know what you want to present, then find what it takes to make it work. There are numerous books and computer-based help products that can assist you in this process. Develop a clear vision for the product you wish to develop and establish milestones to reach that goal.

Your idea may reside in a product that currently exists. Borrowing ideas from proven success stories is a great way to begin. If you have been inspired by a colorful presentation with properly applied music and graphics, then imitate. Imitation is the sincerest form of flattery. However, be careful not to imitate too much. Be original with your content and implementation and do not plagiarize.

Examining the Products

The products that are used in the creation of multimedia projects are numerous and varied. A close examination of what you are going to produce will dictate what external devices or products you will need. Careful planning means that you know the final outcome of your production. Therefore, knowing the end result will tell you which products are required for the production.

Video, photographs, sound, music, animation, computer graphics, and more will play a part in the make-up of your multimedia projects. It is up to you and your project requirements as to which you will have to master.

The beginner knows what he wants but knowing how to get there may be a difficult journey. If you need to produce illustrations for your production and you are not an illustrator, how do you learn which software product is the best for printed media as well as on-screen multimedia production? For incorporating photographic images, what software will allow color adjustments and corrections to make the production look the best for on-screen presentation? For text, what is the best type style, color, and size for the presentation? This is just the beginning. There are many issues that must be addressed during production.

Determining the Audience

Knowing your audience is probably the most important factor in planning your project. After all, you do not have a need to develop unless you have an audience. The tools that you will use as well as the method you will use to develop the project will be determined by the audience.

Will your project be intended for in-house training, product marketing, or mass production and distribution to the public? Will it have to be compatible with different types of computers? These issues must be addressed before you begin development.

You can look forward to the fact that the more you learn about and are involved with multimedia, each new project will be easier, due to the experience that is gained from each. Each project will also add to your total skill set. For example, if you produce a project that incorporates photography, animation, and video, then you will be able to carry over these skills to your next project. Not only that, but with each new project, you will have better ideas on design and implementation. A refreshing part of expanding your current skill set is that with each new venture, you will have substantial experience from which to draw.

When determining your target audience, another aspect that must be addressed is funding. The time and resources that it takes to develop a multimedia presentation or product will vary with each circumstance. If a production is being developed for an in-house function, then it may be a part of your job to produce it, meaning that the production cost is buried in company overhead. If you are producing a multimedia product for distribution to the mass market, then the constraints are quite different. Developing a mass-marketed product could mean hundreds of thousands of dollars in advance. Therefore, when you predict an estimated completion time, management usually expects that the product will be finished and that the funds are sufficient to complete the job.

Each project is unique, and preplanning is essential towards reaching a finalized product as well as to effectively reach an audience.

Creating It Yourself
Versus Using Predesigned

There are many options to consider when producing a multimedia related product. All of the elements that make up a multimedia production can be produced with your own resources if you possess the proper skill set for creating the variety of graphic and sound related files, and if you have access the required hardware products. If you are a novice and do not have access to all of the equipment or software for production, there are other avenues that will allow you to develop your product.

In the early days of personal computing, placing a graphic image into a word processing document was somewhat revolutionary. At this point, electronic clip art was developed. Many companies came into existence for the sole purpose of developing predesigned graphic elements for specific applications. Like traditional clip art services for producing advertising art or publication art, this clip art consisted of electronic files that were ready to copy and paste into your word processing or page layout document (see Figure 2.2). Clip art quickly became popular due to the demand for high-quality artwork for print and presentation.

Figure 2.2 Clip-art samples from Image Club Graphics.

Figure 2.3 Clip media consists of a variety of source material.

Today, this concept has expanded from clip art to clip media. This is due to the fact that the concept now includes predesigned art, animation, sound, photographs, and video images, that can be purchased and used in projects. Typically, if you purchase this form of media, they are considered license free. This means that when you purchase the product, you have legal permission to use and distribute without being required to pay royalties to any party. If you choose to use a video clip from a commercial video title in your production, however, beware. This information is protected by copyright laws. Never use copyrighted material. Look for an applicable product in a royalty-free package or create your own.

Some companies specialize in the development and distribution of clip media that include a variety of media types on CD-ROM. A typical product could include 1,000 stock photographs, 100 live-action video clips, and 1,000 sound effect and music clips. All of this information is royalty-free and prices start around $50. This media can be extremely helpful when time and creative resources are at a minimum. It is difficult to conceive how much time would go into developing or acquiring this information on your own.

Whether you use your own designs or clipmedia, most presentations contain numerous support files. Oftentimes many of these files are variations of a common file. A graphic could be used for one part of a presentation, then be slightly modified and used once again later. They often contain almost the same name and look almost identical. These files become numerous and can create confusion when trying to locate them for use in your production. Using a visual database can be very beneficial here.

Figure 2.3 demonstrates how various types of files are available for instant access. By using a visual database such as Adobe Fetch, you can see a thumbnail of the file for easy reference. These files can be created by the user, or can be taken from a clip-media resource. When working with multimedia projects, the external files can be numerous. Using a visual database like Fetch allows you to quickly find the file you are looking for.

Choosing the Complexity

As you may have noticed, there are some very exciting CD-ROM titles currently available on the market that provide excellent content and presentation. These titles are fulfilling their intended purpose by providing sophisticated sound, graphics, and spectacular integration of storytelling and interactivity. Most commercially available products are designed by experienced multimedia developers. However, since this is still a relatively new field, you may not be that far behind. As a novice, you can learn about the process of development. All it takes is time and training on the appropriate software to make it all work together. Your adaptability to these skills will rely on your creativity, time, and interest in the necessary processes.

If you have ever used a page layout program, such as Adobe PageMaker, you know that these programs are

Figure 2.4 Page layout programs and multimedia presentation programs both accept a variety of prepared media files.

designed to receive various elements that have been prepared by other software programs. These programs are very sophisticated but are not designed as a universal solution for creating all of the elements that typically are a part of a page. Elements that are placed into these page layout programs consist of the following:

- Illustrations from a drawing/illustration program

- Text from a word processing program

- Photographs from a scanner

- Charts from charting software

- Line art from clip-art programs

These page layout programs offer sophistication in the following areas:

- Accept a variety of file formats: .pct, .tif, .eps, .bmp, .gif, and others

- Allow the resizing of graphic elements

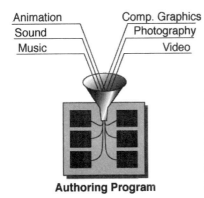

Animation
Sound
Music
Comp. Graphics
Photography
Video

Authoring Program

Figure 2.5
All of the elements that make up a multimedia presentation are placed into the authoring program.

- Provide precision text features such as leading, kerning, horizontal scale adjustment, tracking, etc.

- Adjust tone, texture, and line-screening of scanned images

- Rotate images

These are just a few of the features that these programs offer.

As previously mentioned, page layout programs typically cannot create the scan, line art, chart, or logo, but are well equipped to have various file types placed into them, and to output the file with excellent results. This is what they are designed to do (see Figure 2.4).

This concept is somewhat similar to the process of multimedia development. Programs like Macromedia Director are parallel to page layout programs. Some authoring environments do not have the capability to produce movies, scans, sound, etc., but rather accept all of these files and allow you to coordinate all of them into an orchestrated scheme to interact appropriately at the time you want them to (see Figure 2.5).

Design and Your Skill Set

As you journey into the multimedia arena, you will find that design is a fundamental consideration. Design will apply to many phases of multimedia presentation development. Design is used in the creation of art, sound, animation, video, computer graphics, and all of the support items in a production (see Figure 2.6). Design sometimes refers to the manner in which the pieces are put together, such as the way a presentation will be displayed, on what products, and in what environment. All of these aspects reflect design considerations.

It will not take you very long to realize that there are a lot of issues to be addressed in multimedia planning and execution. This may bring you to the issue of focusing on what constitutes your current skill set. For example, you may be an excellent graphic artist, having mastered the graphic design process on the computer. Because of your skills in this discipline, you may be an excellent candidate to learn the necessary software to totally author a multimedia project. But remember, there are a lot of disciplines involved in the overall multimedia development process other than just graphic design. On the other hand, your present job description may dictate that it is just not feasible for you to dedicate the time required to become a master of all processes.

Each situation will vary. If you are a student wishing to learn all of the disciplines, then you will need exposure to each process, and therefore develop a degree of proficiency in each. If you want to learn this technology/art form as a course of study or to develop a new business, then you will also need to expand your existing skill set.

Having hands-on experience is the best teacher. The more multimedia components you can be involved with, the better qualified you will be to create, produce, and present, using these tools.

Figure 2.6 Authoring programs like Macromedia Director allow the importation of various types of files.

Help from Outside Contractors

With the popularity of multimedia continuing to flourish, an increasing number of companies and individuals are playing a part in the process. One area that is rapidly growing is the number of specialty companies that produce support services. These companies can develop customized media for your productions.

Very much like the clip-media services mentioned earlier, these companies can take on the task of producing content-specific media. For example, if you need video footage of a specific sports team that you are planning to use in your production, and you do not have the equipment or expertise to acquire it on your own, these companies' services could provide the footage. This process could also apply to custom photography, sound, animation, three-dimensional graphics, graphic design, the mastering and reproduction of CD-ROMS, and other services.

Growth of these types of support companies occurred during the desktop publishing revolution. Numerous support-related industries, previously not in existence, were developed to support the explosion of this dynamic industry. Based on the fact that multimedia is still in its infancy, the same changes will apply to this fast changing industry.

Making Multimedia Meet Your Needs without Changing Your Job Description

Multimedia development is a full-time job in many instances. However, if you need media support for various forms of presentation design, how can you get it without becoming a full-time multimedia developer?

Much of the answer lies in the ideas mentioned earlier about who your audience is. If you are on the road giving presentations on a regular basis, a part of your job is to develop presentations. Preparing these presentations could be solely your responsibility. In that case, you must rely on the resources you have available. If your business is to present on-screen facts and statistics with charts and graphs, then a presentation program like Microsoft PowerPoint is a good development tool. If your presentation requires video integration, animation, and other resources that you do not have access to on the road, then you must be able to access them through a local source or from support back at the office. As you can see from this scenario, the issues at hand are knowing what your skills are and utilizing other support mechanisms to execute your presentation or project.

Another scenario would be involvement in a product for distribution on CD-ROM or the Internet. This type of production involves many disciplines and more man hours than organizing a presentation to a live audience. If you are in charge of producing this type of product, then your job description will be that of a manager, controlling the project as a whole. Few individuals are capable of creating an interactive CD-ROM, with all of its elements, by themselves. Again, knowledge of the overall process and what it takes to make it happen is crucial to the organization of such an effort.

Ongoing Development

If you are going to be the producer of the project then you must have a combination of a good imagination and the ability to think through the production processes of the project. Your responsibility is to process your ideas into a logical step-by-step production schedule, complete with all of the peripheral devices required to make the production happen. You also must consider arranging the proper personnel to perform and develop various segments.

Once you have successfully gone through all of the steps in a production, your subsequent projects will be better. This experience will give a freshness to each new project, allowing the creative process to flourish, and the mechanical aspect to become somewhat routine.

Chapter Three

Developing a Project

Who will do it?

How much time will it take?

How much will it cost?

What system will be used?

Will it go "on the road"?

These are a few of the issues you may be facing as you begin the process of developing a multimedia project.

Development scenarios for multimedia projects are broad and will vary based on the nature of the project. As mentioned earlier, to proceed on a productive path, it is very important to know who your audience is. Multimedia projects, no matter how simple or complex, do not have to incorporate all of the resources available to be considered a true multimedia production. A combination of just one or two of these elements will constitute a multimedia project. Your particular level of expertise should not hinder you from developing what is considered a multimedia project, and your knowledge and resources will grow as you learn more about the technology and how to integrate all of the resources that are involved.

Examining the Scope of the Project

A multimedia production can be as simple as a slide show on your computer, using still images only. Sophistication can be given to your project by the addition of voice or animation to the project at a later date. Adding the proper sound at the right time can provide powerful impact, but adding the wrong sound at the wrong time could spell disaster for the message you are trying to convey in your presentation.

Project Definition

What are you producing and for whom are you producing? What is the delivery platform? What is the budget? What multimedia elements will the project include? What development software and hardware is required? When does it have to be finished? There are many questions to answer during the development cycle. Examine each area carefully and come to a solid understanding of each one. This will ensure that you are on the right track towards developing a successful project.

No matter how it will be presented, having a clear picture of the overall project is necessary to produce any type or size multimedia product. To truly capture this picture, careful examination of the project, and the development of an organizational model is important.

The following topics represent a model that will encompass almost all of the steps necessary when developing any size production. Keep in mind that this list is comprehensive and some elements will not concern smaller projects.

Outline Preparation

Outlining is absolutely necessary to produce any type of presentation. We are all used to outlining in one form or another. Some of us do it in our heads, logically organizing information so that it can be played back on demand, either verbally or mechanically. Others look at schedules and organizational tools and use them in a manner that is either most efficient or most convenient to support whatever process that has to happen.

Outlining, as a tool for preparing and organizing a multimedia project, can be performed in a variety of ways. To organize thoughts, information, and interactivity flow, writing or typing this information will work. This may be done in word processing software. Some applications, such

Figure 3.1 A presentation outline as developed in Microsoft PowerPoint

as Microsoft Word, have an outlining mode built in. This feature allows you to input ideas and thoughts, then arrange them in a logical format.

Most presentation software programs have outlining capabilities built in. This feature allows you to type ideas into an outliner and to easily rearrange the information into a logical formation. Once this is done, the information can be converted into a slide show format, illustrating your text with backgrounds, color, transitions, and animation. This is a good way to begin, and provides a quick method of having your information displayed in a graphical format. From here, you can progressively build a presentation or project. Figure 3.1 shows an example of an outline developed in Microsoft PowerPoint.

For multimedia applications, an important concept is to develop a prototype or an outline to determine if the idea that you have for your production can be translated into a workable product. This prototype would best be developed in the authoring software that you will use for your final product. The prototype will also give a feel for how the final product will be designed and operated. This is also important for developing the human interface of the product. This type of outlining is much more visual, and will take some of the in-between steps out of the traditional outlining approach. Outlining in a software environment, by creating a dummy screen, is usually for those who are very familiar with their presentation/authoring software of choice. This type of outlining crosses into the storyboarding process.

Storyboarding

A storyboard is simply a visual representation of the different frames, or screens, that will be included in your production. The purpose of a storyboard is to visualize how the story will flow, and to ensure that no vital information is left out during the sometimes confusing development process. If your product is going to be interactive, requiring that others have decisions to make, then the storyboard will be helpful for determining when and where user input can or should happen. In this situation, many options must be reviewed to make sure the flow of information reacts to the user as intended by the developer. Storyboards are helpful, if not mandatory, for even the smallest project, and are crucial for large projects involving many production team players

Before developing a storyboard, the outline process should be completed. The project developer or producer will embellish the outline even further by developing a storyboard (see Figure 3.2).

Storyboards let you know what will happen in each frame, and the content that needs to be acquired or developed for each. Storyboards can be done on paper utilizing the ever popular stick figure, or can be done in presentation

Figure 3.2 A storyboard is critical to the creation of a coherent flow of information.

software such as PowerPoint or mPower, or in authoring software, such as Director. There are also specific software applications designed especially for storyboarding.

An advantage of developing the storyboard in the final authoring or presentation environment is that features such as graphics, interactivity, "hot buttons," and other integral elements can be gradually built upon. As this building process continues, and modifications and improvements are made, eventually the final product will evolve. Make sure that the authoring program supports screen printing or page printing. This will be necessary to produce a hard copy for distribution and proofing.

Interface Development

In multimedia terminology, the interface refers to what the user sees on a screen. In a kiosk environment, for example, the user interface is the information on the screen that is seen, heard, and touched. The same is true for an interactive presentation or computer-based training application. The interface is a person-to-screen interaction. An interface traditionally applies to one of these situations,

Figure 3.3 This graphic is an example of an interactive presentation interface.

and almost always refers to the way the user interacts with the screen.

If your multimedia project is designed for multiple users, an easy to use interface should be implemented. For example, if you are designing an interactive kiosk, requiring that the user make selections by touching a button on the screen, then the screen images should be clean and uncluttered (see Figure 3.3). If the product is an interactive presentation viewed on a computer screen then the buttons and/or options should be designed in a manner that is logical, easy to read, and visually leads the user to specific areas. If the product is a computer-based presentation being shown to a room full of people, then what they see should be designed clearly and concisely.

Developing an interface screen usually involves creating artwork, buttons, and other elements with a drawing or painting software program. The interface art can be

```
Date:     3/18/98
Channel: 04
On:       8:00 pm
Off:      9:00 pm
```

Figure 3.4   The VCR has become easier to program, thanks to refinements in the interface.

designed in a graphics program and the interactivity implemented in the authoring software.

The interface is important in any phase of multimedia development, but is most important when your product demands that others interact with it. Some books are easy to read and some are not, based on who is telling the story and the words they use. The same is true for computer-based presentations. If your product requires interactivity, users should be able to easily interact with it. Ease of interaction should not be based on how it works for you, but how it works for others. Testing by others will provide valuable insight as to how your product will work for a general audience.

The interface is usually not the information that you are trying to communicate, but rather the shell that allows you to approach the information. This shell can affect the outcome of retrieving information. The interface screen is what the user sees and uses to navigate through a product or presentation. If the information being communicated is good, and the interface poor, then the overall product will be negatively affected.

Early VCRs offered basic features, such as speed control, remote controls, and the ability to set a timer to record a program at a user specified time. These proved to be difficult to program. Today's VCRs provide straightforward, on-screen menus for programming. This is due to the fact that manufacturers have listened to consumer suggestions and have made this process much more user friendly (see Figure 3.4).

Interface issues have also surrounded the way we gain access to the Internet. This process is also becoming easier due to the graphical user interface that is being utilized by most Internet browsers.

Hardware and Software Decisions

There are countless hardware and software products currently on the market and more are added on a daily basis. Each new project you produce will have its own unique hardware and software requirements. Developing a presentation for a one-time showing to an audience will require different hardware and software than that required to develop a CD-ROM. Choosing hardware and software will be affected by the type of project, the budget, the time-frame, the equipment on hand, and other factors.

Figure 3.5 demonstrates some typical projects and the unique requirements of each. Note that each scenario will utilize some common equipment, but each process requires something unique. This is because each instance addresses a situation in a new venue, therefore requiring new hardware to successfully convey information.

You may be in a situation that demands that you utilize your existing equipment however inadequate you feel it may be for the job. This is when creativity and outside resources come into play. There are some definite requirements that must be met in order to perform certain tasks. For example, to simply use a presentation program, like Adobe Persuasion, your computer must have the following minimum configuration:

Minimum System	RAM	Minimum Hard Disk Space
Windows 3.1w/Intel 486	8MB	20MB
Macintosh w/System 7.0	8MB	20MB

In the realm of multimedia presentation and production, working with the minimum is like treading on thin ice. To clarify this point, consider the following scenario. Your computer has the minimum amount of random-access

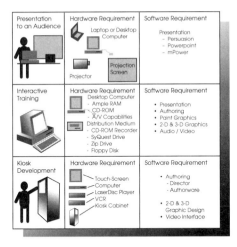

Figure 3.5 Each type of production requires different hardware and software support. This figure demonstrates some of the differences.

memory (RAM) required by the software manufacturer. This allows you to develop a presentation. But, let us say that you have a large presentation with sixty-five different screens. You work hard making your text look great. Your backgrounds are in place, you have placed numerous scanned graphics into your presentation, and all is well. As you proceed to present your masterpiece, you notice that your presentation begins to get sluggish and as you advance from frame to frame, each one takes longer to display on screen. You are presenting to an audience and you haven't rehearsed it. You find that you are stuttering and stammering while you wait for the slides to load. You have struggled through the presentation and are now ready to present your last slide. This slide contains a very large, beautiful scanned image which contains the heart of your presentation. You advance to the slide and your system crashes. You haven't backed up your file and are not sure that it is salvageable. You are embarrassed because your visual is not there to deliver the "punch" you anticipated. What happened? You needed more RAM! But, how were you to know? After all, you followed the suggested minimum that the manufacturer recommended.

What happened here is that the user was simply inexperienced. Even though manufacturers recommend a minimum configuration, it is not optimum, or even workable, when you load the program to the max. In the multimedia world, you work with large graphics, video, audio, animation, and other files, that use a great deal of RAM. Not only do these programs vie for RAM, but they love disk space as well. Beware of manufacturers' suggested minimums. They will work but you must know the minimum and maximum loads they are capable of carrying. Furthermore, pay close attention to the label which says to allot a certain amount of RAM to the application. If you have 8 MB of RAM total, be aware that the operating system will consume a certain portion of that in order to function. On the Macintosh, the operating system alone could consume as much as 4 MB of RAM. This leaves 4 MB for other applications. In the multimedia world, this will not produce much (see Figure 3.6).

Consideration must also be given to the amount of disk space you have available. Word processing or spreadsheet applications consume a minimum amount of space on your hard disk drive compared to the space needed for graphic, sound, and video files. Careful consideration must be given to your storage system. Prices for hard disk space, and external storage devices are very reasonable, making the cost of expanding your systems capabilities affordable.

If speed and efficiency are important and you are using an older, slower system, you should upgrade your system. Like storage devices, computer systems now offer more power and features than ever before, and high-speed systems can be integrated easier than ever before. If you are going to produce high-level media on a consistent basis, you should upgrade to newer technology. It will pay for itself in a short period just in time savings. It will also help in the sanity area, as you are trying to make all of the media components work in harmony.

Figure 3.6 Knowing where you stand with your memory availability is critical as you begin to work in multimedia environments.

This upgrading concept also applies to the software arena. Acquiring the right product for specific needs is essential. Purchasing software that will allow import and export features is critical. A key element in multimedia computing is knowing the software that will make your project work and knowing your options as to where you can take your information. Is it compatible with other systems? Is it a well known program that will be around tomorrow? Can I export it into other applications? There are many issues that need to be addressed as new software products are acquired.

Output Format

A multimedia presentation designed for a one-time showing could be confined to floppy disk, a Zip disk, CD-ROM, or perhaps an internal hard disk drive. These types of projects will probably be archived if they will fit on floppies or a cartridge drive, but if your presentation is valuable, you will not want to leave it on a hard disk drive. First, they take up a lot of space and second, the failure rate is potentially high, especially if the drive is in daily use.

Your final output format will usually be based on what your presentation is and where it has to go. For large productions you will want to store these on high-capacity media such as a ZIP disk, a magneto-optical disk, a CD-ROM, or a DVD-ROM.

Production Cycle

The following topics demonstrate a suggested scenario to follow for the production of a project such as a commercial CD-ROM title for mass distribution, or perhaps a Website. The outline, though comprehensive, will be helpful for all projects.

Prototypes

By developing prototypes early in the design and planning stages of any project, the projected workflow and process planning will crystallize, allowing the project to come together faster. Test in small segments and on planned intervals so that you know where you are in the production stage.

Organizing a Team

Once your prototype is developed, you must consider the team players that will be involved in the overall production. This applies to almost any size project. You will need to assign various tasks to team managers. These managers will need to be responsible for specific segments of the production. Examples of such managers are designers, videographers, programmers, and artists.

Product Design

If there is a need to develop a presentation or product, then the steps to take will be logical. As architect Frank Lloyd Wright said, "Form follows function." By the time you make it to the product design stage, you may have to rethink and rework your original storyboard. At this stage, you should have a good feel as to the amount of time, resources, and cost of development your production will require. This process should become easier with future projects.

Testing for Usability

The best source of feedback on project development is user testing. Your ideas are important and critical to the overall development process, but having someone unfamiliar with the project give an objective opinion is invaluable. This usability testing should occur on a scheduled basis during the development process. One of the worst things that could happen is that you reach near completion of your project and then invite testers only to find out that you left out a critical step. Going back at this time is truly a setback. Plan ahead.

Product Redesign and Modifications

Based on the valuable input received from the previous step, you will find that you will tweak your production continuously during development, keeping in mind your original target date for completion. Make sure that your revisions are in accordance with your schedule. Redesign activities demand time management skills on behalf of the project manager. If time management is not your strong suit, then assign this task to a capable team member.

Financial Considerations

The financial consideration of developing and producing a sophisticated multimedia project is a critical part of the process. In any project, it can be costly to get to the stage of developing a prototype to demonstrate. Financial issues are also an integral part of marketing, testing, and distributing. Each of these areas require serious consideration.

Since this is still a new field, there are not a great deal of outside resources that can assist you by providing an exact cost model of what your custom project will cost. This will demand more time and consideration during the initial planning stages. All phases must be carefully calculated and one must plan for the unexpected.

Final Organization and Team Implementation

At this point, you are ready to take another look at your team and perhaps adjust the players that will assist in the preparation of your product or project. These players may or may not be people within your organization or even immediately at your disposal. Players could be resources or providers in the form of vendors, local service bureaus, or contractual support.

Media Production/Software Development

Making multimedia work really begins with the successful merging of the various media types with the proper software implementation. The media (video, graphics, scans, artwork, sound effects, audio), and the software (the authoring environment that makes the media come alive), must be developed in harmony to ensure the success of your production.

Management skills are important at this stage. The need for tight organization during the development of the various media types is required. In all projects, production deadlines are critical. Obviously, final software development and assembly cannot take place until all of the externals are completed.

Product Documentation

Products designed for distribution to a marketplace must contain documentation. As a project develops, required documentation could take on a variety of forms.

With computer-based presentations designed for personal use there is traditionally no requirement for documentation. If it is, for example, a corporate presentation that others will use, then the documentation format could consist of a file or notes that are a part of the presentation preparation. This information could be a separate file, and be considered speaker's notes or other types of notes related to the presentation content. With interactive titles, games, educational titles, and more, documentation takes the shape of pertinent support material for the program. There is so much detail that goes into these products, the issue of providing the user with the necessary information to find out what they need to know, when they need to know it, is critical.

Print has been the traditional form of documentation in the past. However, in this electronic age, other methods of preparing product documentation are feasible. Many programs offer on-line help files. These files reside in the application and offer instant support. Another method of support documentation would be to provide an electronic file with the program. This file may be a text document that is shipped on the same storage media as the program. These files are traditionally called "read me" files. These files can be read by your word processing program or your program may include a basic "reader" application, allowing access without the need for additional applications.

A popular method for reading documents on a variety of platforms is a Portable Document Format file (PDF). This is a format developed by Adobe Systems. Saving in the PDF format will ensure that anyone can read and print the documentation on any computer system, providing he has a copy of the Acrobat Reader software. The Adobe Acrobat Reader application can be freely distributed with files saved in the PDF format, allowing access to the information by the user.

Along with developing a multimedia product and bringing it to completion, preparing support documentation is critical. Support documentation is its own unique project, requiring production organization, art preparation,

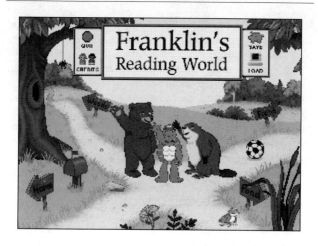

Figure 3.7 Packaging plays an important part in the marketing and distribution of commercial software.

formation of a layout format, and the actual printing or output process. Like a multimedia project, documentation will go through many redesigns and checkpoints before the final product is ready. One good thing about producing a CD-ROM project for distribution is that much of the text traditionally printed can be on the disk, potentially eliminating the need for extensive printed materials. We have not quite reached the paperless society, but with current technologies many options are available.

Packaging

For commercial projects, packaging considerations are very important. After all, the package is the first thing a consumer will see and therefore will create a positive or negative impression of your product. Packaging concerns often play a part in the mock-up phase of product development as well.

Packaging design, like most art forms, follows the wave of contemporary trends. Consider what will make your product stand out from the competition.

Advertising

Advertising is imperative for commercial media products. To get your product out to the masses requires promotional literature or even a working prototype available for advanced showings. This may also require promotional packaging and documentation.

Another form of advertising is to produce demonstration versions of a product or presentation. These demo versions are a great way to allow your target audience to view a selected portion of your product before purchasing. If your product is what the marketplace is waiting for, these demo versions should generate a positive response.

Final Product and Testing

At this point, you are at the final stage of your production. Once you are here, no matter how hard you and your team have worked, be prepared to find flaws. When you do, run your product through another round of critical checks.

Feedback from industry professionals on product, packaging, and documentation is also important. These early versions that are shipped out for evaluation are considered Alpha or Beta versions of your product.

Manufacturing Your Product

You should be at this point only after rigorous testing and only after going through every possible scenario of product inconsistency. Now that you know that your product is ready to go into production, let it go. If the product is going to be pressed into a CD-ROM, the initial cost is going to be substantial. However, if you are producing in volume, your individual cost will be nominal. Remember, the nominal cost could turn out to be an enormous cost if the data copied on to the CD is flawed. Know that you have a work-able product before going to press. These procedures will also apply to presentations and products intended for broadcast onto the Internet. If it goes out to the masses, they will let you know in a hurry if there are problems or flaws.

Distributing Your Product

At this point it is time to sit back and enjoy the fruits of your labor. If you have done the job properly, the product will fulfill its intended purpose.

Chapter Four

Choosing Hardware

If you are confused by the rapid growth of hardware choices in the marketplace, you are not alone. There are about as many options in computer hardware and peripheral devices as there are stars in the sky. However, in the scope of this book, we are specifically focusing on the devices and products that surround multimedia production on either Macintosh or Windows computers.

Oftentimes your choice of a multimedia development system will be based on what you are familiar with, what you currently have, or what your research tells you will work best for your desired result. Our goal is to provide an objective review of computer platforms, to discuss the requirements of multimedia computing, and to review common features.

One thing that has become prevalent recently is the convergence of computer technologies and harmony between hardware and software vendors. This is partly due to development integrity by software and peripheral developers, and the strategic alliances between Apple and IBM. This is also due to the mixed hardware environment in corporate America. There are more and more demands for the same software to be available on multiple platforms. There will probably never be just one platform, but the work process will become increasingly similar between systems.

Technologies Introduced through Apple's Macintosh

The Macintosh has always been a media-oriented machine. Since its introduction in 1984, it has always been pitched as a computer that works with other media types. Even though this media may have initially been clip art, it was a start. Apples initial marketing campaigns illustrated the integration of graphics into text (see Figure 4.1). As far as ease of use, their marketing strategy suggested that if you can "point and click," then you can use the Macintosh.

Through the years, the Macintosh has grown and matured substantially, and has truly revolutionized the personal computer marketplace. One thing the Macintosh has accomplished is the establishment of several niche markets or industries. For example, when laser printers were introduced that included the Adobe PostScript page description language, the desktop publishing revolution was born. PostScript took the information on the computer screen and translated it to commands in the laser printer that made it print exactly what you saw on your screen, only better. This was when the term WYSIWYG (what you see is what you get) was born. This firmly set the Mac as the platform of choice for page layout and design for the printing and publishing industries. In the early 1990s, when Apple developed QuickTime, the desktop video revolution began, thus ushering in the introduction of video to desktop multimedia.

Figure 4.1 Art placed directly into the text, as illustrated through this entire book, is a result of the groundbreaking technology introduced with the advent of the Macintosh, and the cut-and-paste process.

Figure 4.2 Though the computer was small and not very expandable, early Macs were revolutionary.

The Macintosh has always been a fun and easy to use environment. Perhaps the good thing about the Macintosh is that you do not have to know much about computer operation to set up the system and to quickly become a productive user. This environment allows you to take your existing skill set and, with the proper software, get right to work. An example of this is if you know how to type, and are accustomed to working on a typewriter, then using a word processing program on the Mac is extremely easy. Another example is if you are a skilled graphic artist, familiar with painting, drafting, free-hand sketching, and other skills, the translation of your existing skills into this computer environment will be natural. With the growth and sophistication of the Windows operating environment, this easy to use interface is carried over in the same manner.

Running Multimedia

Minimum System for Development

What does it take for multimedia titles to run on a Mac? From a users perspective, having a color system with at least 16 MB of RAM and a 13-inch or 14-inch monitor is a basic start. A CD-ROM drive is not required for multimedia development, but is needed to view other titles and is considered a "standard" device in a multimedia computer.

CD-ROM

Floppy disk drive

16MB RAM

1.0 Gb hard drive

Microphone

14″ monitor

Powered speakers

Figure 4.3 A basic multimedia computer system.

Sound is an important part of multimedia; therefore, speakers are critical. Either internal or external speakers will significantly enhance multimedia presentations.

Even though color and sound quality are nice, they are not necessarily required. This is based on what you are going to develop. There are a multitude of older Macintosh computers that do not have color displays or the sophistication in sound capabilities that today's computers offer. Based on the particular multimedia production you are viewing, hardware considerations are extremely important.

Figure 4.3 shows a basic multimedia development system. Keep in mind that these features are a minimum environment. You can enhance each aspect of this suggestion as far as your need and budget allow you to. You can make it as elaborate as you desire. These suggestions apply for Macintosh or PC.

Preferred Models for Media Development

If you are in a start-up situation, and have a liberal equipment budget, there are certain systems that will handle any job. One thing to remember is that most computers

EXPANDABILITY OPTIONS TO CONSIDER FOR NEW EQUIPMENT		
Product	**Minimum**	**Expansion Options**
Memory	Minimum 16	Expandable to 256 and above
Expansion Slots	PCI	2 to 3
Microprocessor	Must be upgradeable	
Hard Drive	500 MB	2–4 Gigabyte recommended
CD-ROM	2X speed	8X + recommended

Table 4.1 Most computers can be upgraded in some way.

today are very expandable. They can be expanded by adding more RAM, larger hard disk drives, and peripherals to enhance functioning. Table 4.1 demonstrates some expansion options.

Hardware Considerations When Shopping for Software

If you own a computer or have the responsibility to purchase software for computers, then you are familiar with the constraints of software shopping. If you see a software title that you are considering purchasing, the first question you ask is, "Will it run on my computer?" This means you must investigate to see if it is compatible with Macintosh, DOS, or Windows Multimedia Personal Computer (MPC). This is where the software issue becomes a hardware issue. However, just knowing this is not enough. Oftentimes there are many other requirements to ensure that the software will work on your machine. Software developers typically tell you exactly what is required to run their product by printing the requirements right on the box.

MACINTOSH
SYSTEM REQUIREMENTS
  LCIII or higher
  4 MB of RAM
   (8 recommended)
  Hard disk drive
  Speakers
  Mouse
  13" monitor or larger,
   set at 256 colors
  Printer recommended

MINIMUM WINDOWS
REQUIREMENTS
  Intel 486
  Single-speed CD-ROM
  8-bit color
  Windows 3.1
  8 MB memory
  13" monitor set at
   256 colors
  Speakers

Figure 4.4 Software compatibility requirements.

A typical requirement sticker on the side of a multi-media title is shown in Figure 4.4.

Today, many software products are delivered on CD-ROM. Often, both Windows and Macintosh versions are contained on the same CD-ROM, therefore, it is becoming more common to see requirements for both Windows and Macintosh computers on the same box .

Developing Multimedia

If you are developing media for distribution to the masses, you must first determine on which machines you desire to make your product compatible. You can develop a product that will work with more recent models, containing faster processors and perhaps more RAM, however, if you want to reach all computer users, you may want to consider making a version for the earlier machines as well.

If you decide to go the route of providing a version of your product that is compatible with all older systems, you will need to access other computers for testing. This could require that you have access to everything from the original Macintosh 128 to the current version of the Power Macintosh; from an old 286 system to the latest Intel-based processor. For example, if your production is to be compatible with all Mac or Windows systems ever made, much homework and preparation must be made to ensure that the product will be compatible with the variety of screen resolutions and sizes, hardware configurations, system software versions, and storage media, just to mention a handful of considerations. This would be a monumental undertaking.

DOS/Windows Integration into the Macintosh

The Macintosh has had the capability to read DOS files for quite some time. With the introduction of the Macintosh IIx, in 1988, Apple included a new floppy disk drive called the "super-drive." This unit was revolutionary because it read the new high-density disk, which held 1.4 MB of data. This significantly aided the need to save more information on a single floppy disk. At the time, applications and file sizes were on the increase, demanding more storage space. The drive also had the capability to read disks that were formatted for Apple II systems (ProDOS) format, and disks formatted for DOS-based systems.

At this point, accessing software from different machines was not commonplace, but this technology allowed users to import files such as spreadsheet data created in a DOS based spreadsheet program directly into the Macintosh for importation into a Mac-based spreadsheet. This was also applicable to other file types, such as typed documents created in a word processor and graphic file translation.

If you are a Macintosh user and have a need to run Windows based applications, how do you do it? One option is to use a software program that allows the Macintosh to emulate the DOS, or Windows, operating system. This allows you to use DOS or Windows applications right on your Macintosh. From a hardware perspective, it is important to know that Macintosh models equipped with "super-drives" will accept DOS-formatted disks. This is required if you want to load DOS-related software disks into a Macintosh. The super-drive, which is still a Macintosh standard

Figure 4.5 Some of us use our computer for just one reason: as a word processor, for spreadsheets, or for database information.

today, allows access to 400k single-sided disk, 800k double-sided disk, and 1.4 MB high-density disks. If your Mac is a Macintosh IIx or newer it has the super-drive built in, allowing you to read each of these disk types.

Another option for running DOS/Windows on a Macintosh is to purchase an additional hardware product. By purchasing an add-on board for your Macintosh, you can emulate the PC environment with the power of a real computer. These boards use your disk drives, monitors, and printer, thus allowing you the capabilities of a full functioning DOS/Windows system right in your Macintosh. This is a good solution; however, with the price of some of these units, you could almost afford to purchase a complete Windows system.

What You Must Know

There are several things you must know about hardware. For example, you must know the significant differences in Macintosh and Windows multimedia hardware. You must know the hardware componentry that allows the integration of the various media types. You must know the

Figure 4.6 Some of us want to use the computer for all we can get out of it. Is this the vision of how AV and multimedia technologies are merged?

peripheral devices that physically connect to a computer system to enhance its capabilities. You must have an understanding of presenting information on equipment other than a personal computer. You must have an understanding of the various array of storage devices and how they work. To actively participate in multimedia computing, this knowledge is essential.

The Technical Mindset of the User

Anyone can do multimedia, but with any process, there are varying degrees of what you can do. What you can do is based on a variety of conditions. Some of these conditions include: how much time you have to dedicate to the process, the resources you have (the computer, software, and technical assistance), and what you want to do with it. Your adeptness and willingness to learn what this is all about is also an important aspect.

Having an inquisitive mindset about the products and processes will also be beneficial. The specifics of hardware and software change almost daily. Making an effort to keep up with the latest products and trends will enhance your involvement as you strive to stay on the cutting edge. Reading technical and trade publications are tremendously helpful to stay current.

AV Technologies

It used to be that computer owners used their computers for one specific purpose. An example of this would be the way that PC owners began to replace the typewriter as the device of choice for typing and producing letters and other forms of communication. Others used their computers primarily for spreadsheets, a database, or other specific purpose.

As the capabilities of personal computers grew in sophistication, they began to serve as a comprehensive solution for a variety of tasks. Today, we are beginning to use our computer systems for much more than just word processing or spreadsheets, or other linear tasks. Contemporary computer systems offer a host of new capabilities from year to year.

An example of this is the way that we use our system for e-mail or to access the Internet. This allows communication to the world in a format other than the telephone using our computer as the interface device. The way this is possible is by having telephone capabilities built in the computer. By having phone capabilities built in, we are able to send and receive fax transmissions through our machines. This is fantastic technology, which allows on-screen documents to be sent without requiring the creation of a hard copy. This also works in reverse. Fax transmissions can be received directly into the computer and printed only if needed.

Even though the connection to modems and general telecommunications has been around a while, there are new audio/video capabilities being added to personal computers. Apple calls this "AV Technologies," and they have been a part of their computer line since 1993. Since that time, it has become commonplace for computer hardware vendors to bundle such features with their computer products. As far as manufacturers of Intel-based PCs, these features come under the componentry typical to the MPC label. A system labeled as a Multimedia Personal Computer would include these features as a standard part of their hardware configuration. Following is a review of some of these features.

Telecommunications

Integrating data, fax, answering machine, and telephone into the computer is commonplace today. With the necessity to connect to voice, facsimile, and the Internet, the computer and phone are integral components. These features, being essential communication elements, add a level of sophistication to the typical computer system. These features also enhance the ability to gather and distribute media components.

Video and Graphics Input and Output (I/O)

This is the ability to capture video from a wide variety of sources such as VCRs, digital cameras, video cameras, and laserdiscs, and then output it to other sources. With the proper software, such as Apple's QuickTime extension, video can be displayed in a window on the monitor, similar to any other computer document. Like other windows, the video image can be resized, usually from the size of a postage stamp up to a full-screen image. This technology also contains the ability to capture images displayed on the screen. This can be done by using frame grabbing techniques. Frame grabbing is capturing a frame randomly during playback, or "freezing" the image, then grabbing, in order to capture specific images.

Computers with AV/MPC capabilities have the ability to send information to other peripheral devices. For instance, if you want to copy a computer presentation onto videotape, VCR-type connectors are included allowing connection to a VCR for taping. This process is also used for connection from the computer to a television, or other

Figure 4.7 A QuickTime movie window contains the movie and offers typical controls like: play, pause, forward, and reverse.

device, for the presentation of computer-based information. These connections conform to world wide standards like NTSC, PAL, and SECAM video signals. Traditional S-VHS connections are also included in these systems.

QuickTime™

QuickTime is an extension compatible with Macintosh- and Windows- compatible computers, that allows digital video files (or movies), to be played on your computer. QuickTime technology allows information such as sound, video, graphics, and animation to be stored, then used in a variety of applications. The introduction of QuickTime revolutionized the ability to go beyond the static images that traditional computing offered. This also ushered in a new era of enhanced multimedia processes. QuickTime not only has the ability to display video, but offers high quality audio as well.

QuickTime is available for both Macintosh and Windows environments. QuickTime is not a traditional software application, but rather an extension that allows the computer to recognize files saved in this format to be played back.

Speech Technology

Not only can your computer speak to you, you can also speak to your computer. Speech recognition software has

Figure 4.8 The speech setup window from the Macintosh Control Panels menu.

made great strides in the past few years. Speech technology allows a document to be read to you in your choice of voices. You can also talk to your computer, giving commands that you would traditionally make with a keyboard or a mouse. Speech technology offers tremendous potential in computing. We are also beginning to see it used in other arenas as well.

AV technologies are becoming increasingly popular and are available on Macintosh and Windows environments. This type of trend will probably continue to grow in popularity, and will become increasingly affordable to purchase a system that has these features built in.

The Connection Between Hardware and Multimedia

Phone, fax, audio, video, and other processes are now a part of computing. The ability to integrate or import these processes through a computer is changing the way work and visual communication is performed. In the realm of multimedia development, better processes are available to make any type of production more dynamic. As these components evolve, the way information is produced will change, as well as who is doing the production.

Chapter Five

Choosing Software

As you begin to plan a multimedia project, there are many areas to consider such as your hardware platform, your audience, and the creation process. Perhaps the most important element to consider is the software that you will use to make it happen. Software is like the engine of an automobile: it gets you where you want to go.

Software, like hardware, is subject to change. This usually occurs through regularly scheduled updates. Through software company research, and user input, software products typically get better with each release. If the product is viable, it will enjoy a long life in the marketplace. In multimedia design and development, there are key software players and since multimedia incorporates a variety of media types, interaction with many programs is typical.

There are literally thousands of software products on the market today. One must differentiate between applications and software products. The application is the vehicle for producing a product while the software product is the result of a series of files created by one or more software applications.

An example of a software product are the files created in Adobe Premiere (see Figure 5.1). Premiere is designed to create digital video and audio files. Premiere is a software application that depends heavily on the input of files created in other application programs. Premiere combines these files in a manner that creates a finished software product. In Premiere's case the product is a QuickTime movie. There are other products that follow this pattern.

Figure 5.1
Files placed into Adobe Premiere to create a QuickTime or an .avi movie.

Having a software program that provides a workable multimedia authoring environment can determine the success of your end product. There are numerous software programs on the market today, each with their unique features. What may be a good solution for your development needs may not be appropriate for others. Like everything else, these choices are based on the individual and his unique vision.

If your development needs are going to be fairly basic, then begin with a basic program that provides an intuitive interface, one that can deliver the goods you need without a high learning curve. On the other hand, if your needs require that you develop serious interactive content, or other features that demand considerable extendibility, then by all means invest in the best. Often it is hard to know exactly where your ventures will take you; therefore, it is important to make sure you have a vehicle that can take you wherever you want to go.

As you become involved in producing multimedia content, you may be required to assemble a team to assist in the production of your product. The team configuration will totally be based on the complexity of the particular project. However, if your focus is an in-house presentation, then you could very well pull it off yourself. You may often find yourself playing the role of the entire team. If your product will be a commercially available product, such as a CD-ROM title or a game that will have mass appeal to a vast marketplace, then you will definitely need to assemble a team to perform various tasks during project development.

As with most software products, the more you work with a particular program, the more proficient you become. In the team approach, the demands of having to know all the programs extensively is not required. You may be the idea person, while the graphic or programming person would be another part of the team. If this is your situation, you are in luck. If you are working with a staff of designers that understand the operation of media integration and the scripting process, there are several authoring software programs that will work well.

A software product can be many things: a game, a utility, an interactive presentation, a training program, or one of many other products. These types of products are what constitute the thousands of software products that are on the market. When it comes to software applications, the products that allow the development of files and end products, the number is much smaller.

As mentioned in previous chapters, there are different products and processes that are required to develop multimedia. Along with the hardware required to capture audio, video, computer graphics, animation, and the other processes that make up multimedia, there must be a software product to support each. Table 5.1 provides an overview of some of the software products that support these processes.

Environment	Product	Publisher
Authoring	Director	Macromedia
	Authorware	Macromedia
	mPower	Multimedia Design Corp.
	Quest	Allen Communications
Video Editing	Premiere	Adobe Systems
	Avid VideoShop	Avid Technology, Inc.
Sound Editing	Sound Edit 16	Macromedia
	Deck II	Macromedia

Table 5.1 Software products that support the multimedia process.

Multimedia Authoring:
Macromedia Director

Software Category: Authoring
Platform(s):   Macintosh & Windows
Company: Macromedia

This longtime multimedia workhorse is a real industry staple. Director allows the development of a wide range of presentation types from the very basic to the extremely sophisticated. Director possesses great strength in animation and interactivity. Some authoring software products require that you pay the company a royalty for distributing programs that you have developed using their application. Director allows you to freely distribute any presentation. Director presentations are saved in the form of a Projector file. A projector bundles your presentation with an engine that will play back your presentation on other computers without requiring the Director application.

Figure 5.2 The Score window in Director allows virtually any action to happen based on information entered in the Score Script window.

There are versions of Director for both Macintosh and Windows. Files created on one system can be played on the other system. Director can also be extended through other routines referred to as XObjects. An example of an XObject would be a specific set of commands that would allow the computer to control an external peripheral such as a laserdisc player. A script would be written, perhaps by the manufacturer of the laserdisc player, that would allow Director to access the player. At the proper time, a specified video segment could be retrieved and played.

Director gives you an edge while in the development process. You have the capability to preview any portion of your program during the design process. This includes Lingo scripting. This language is fairly straightforward; however, there is a learning curve. The real advantage of Lingo is the amazing diversity it provides. When using Lingo, learning just a few lines of scripting commands will allow you to develop a wide range of interactivity. Obviously, to accomplish more interactivity and intricacy, more expertise with Lingo will be required. Director contains multiple capabilities that allow team members to use all of the great features, and to quickly pick up where others have left off.

Director also contains a complete set of painting tools to allow both the creation of a graphic object as well as the modification of imported graphics.

Multimedia Presentation Software

For many years, presentations were done mostly by utilizing the old reliable slide projector. Even though the slide projector has made a few changes through the years, the method of inserting a group of slides and advancing one by one has remained the same. This technology has been very effective and will continue to be perhaps the most used form of presentation to an audience.

The effectiveness of a presentation is based on three things:

1. The content presented

2. The quality of the image

3. The effective communication skills of the presenter

As with all presentation techniques, these qualities will waver in their level of importance, making the impact and effectiveness of each presentation unique.

Most of us were raised with the television and other media devices surrounding us. We are accustomed to having bright, colorful images and sound delivered to us through these mediums. Usually, the television can communicate important messages in a short amount of time. For example, the average length of an image displayed on the TV screen during a typical show is only about six seconds. This fast moving pace is set in order to keep our attention. Commercials can throw much more information our way in much less time.

In the world of computer-based presentations and presentation software solutions, we should keep in mind who we are presenting to and what they are expecting to see.

More than likely, the intended audience is expecting to see a message delivered that has some punch.

Early versions of software for computer-based presentations were minimal to say the least. The pioneers in presentation software development offered features like slide-to-slide sequencing, transitions, pop-up text with bullets, and a handful of other effects. Now that the industry has become more sophisticated and more of us are using computer-based presentation software, these programs are fighting to add more features and special effects so that we can stimulate our audience.

As seems to be the norm with most software programs, each release becomes more powerful and feature-packed. Presentation software usually experiences a revision every six months or so with a major version release perhaps every eighteen months.

What exactly do we expect to get out of a presentation program? For many people having the ability to advance from one graphic to another is just fine. All presentation programs will do that. But what about all of the elaborate effects that we see on music videos and in commercials these days? What if your audience demands these types of effects or if your message is to a group that you know will respond better to this type of presentation? Only you can be the judge of what will work best for your particular situation. Remember, you must know who your audience is. This will dictate your presentation method.

The questions above lead us to consider specific software solutions. With so many options out there, where do you begin to qualify what will work best for your situation? It is important to determine what types of presentations you will create and present. Be careful not to purchase a program that will just meet your immediate needs. Keep in mind that the more you learn about the functioning of these programs, the more you will probably do to make your presentations more appealing. An exception to this is if your business is linear, requiring that only a certain procedure be followed with each production. In this case, buy only the essentials that meet your needs.

If you are interested in getting all of the sophisticated features in a presentation program beware of using all of the features in a single presentation. Use good judgment and tasteful design when assembling your production. Too much activity can be distracting to your content.

Most of the software programs contain a host of pre-packaged accessories. These include, but are not limited to auto templates (predesigned backgrounds), context-sensitive help systems, and clip-art file libraries. The more sophisticated programs contain these features as well as: three-dimensional chart creation, video integration, interactivity, animation, and branching. Some of these programs also provide an electronic marker utility. This feature allows the presenter to mark up the computer or presentation screen similar to the way it would be done on an overhead projector with an acetate overlay and color markers.

A new dimension to many presentation programs is the capability to save presentations in a Player format. Like the Projector file mentioned earlier for Director, player files contain enough of the application program to make your presentation play only. This is useful for sending projects to other locations for viewing when they do not own a copy of the original software. A great feature of many of these player files is that they can be authored on the Macintosh and distributed as a Windows compatible file, and vice versa. This capability is becoming standard for most high-end presentation software applications.

Multimedia Necessities

There are certain things that are absolute necessities in multimedia presentation software. These include the ability to accept the following external files:

* Digital Movies—Multimedia presentation software must have the ability to accept movie and sound files that are saved in Apple QuickTime or AVI file format. The integration of digital movie files provides variety and interest to any presentation.

- Sound—Adding background music or narration adds interest and clarification to the message of your presentation. These sound files could be in the form of a voice, music, or sound effect file.

- Animation—Animation can capture and emphasize a point with colorful images and motion. Animation can make the unreal happen and make it believable.

- Charting—Charting is a feature that is used in almost all presentation programs. The most frequent type of presentation given relates to numbers and translates to charted information on dates, growth, and financial issues.

- Interactivity—In early presentation software, about the only form of interactivity was the ability to click the mouse and have the program advance to the next slide. In current programs, much more can happen with your presentation if you choose to make it happen. Hypertext or "hot buttons" can be assigned to various graphics, allowing other actions to happen based on assigned functions. An example of this would be the importation of a digital movie and establishing a command in the program to have the movie play automatically or upon a click of the mouse or other user prompt.

Many so-called presentation software programs offer enough interactive sophistication to function in a kiosk environment. Programs, such as mPower, from Multimedia Design Corporation, offer "hot buttons" for interactive control and "hooks" to external peripherals such as VCRs and laserdisc players.

Some programs allow the integration of many file types. A very important consideration in presentation software is the ability to import the file types that you currently use on a regular basis as well as options for other types that you may use in the future.

As presentation software progresses, look for even more features, easier file integration, and more straightforward point-and-click functions. Another consideration in this arena will also be hardware changes and support for better image and sound quality as well as an improved appearance on screen.

Presentation software should be easy to use and conform to your work style. The ideal presentation software allows the user to concentrate on content development rather than on the mechanical aspects of making it work.

Multimedia Presentation: Microsoft PowerPoint

Software Category: Presentation
Platform(s):   Macintosh & Windows
Company: Microsoft

Microsoft® PowerPoint® presentation graphics program is the industry's most popular presentation graphics application. When PowerPoint 97 was introduced, it was the sixth major release of this popular presentation program. This versatile product offers an easy to use presentation creation environment for the beginner while offering the sophistication needed for experienced presentation designers.

Some PowerPoint features include:

- OfficeArt, animated charts, multimedia clip gallery, clip gallery live (updated images from the Web)

- Professionally designed templates and coordinated color schemes

- Action Buttons to add hyperlinks to other slides

- Improved performance through file compression

- Pre-existing templates for quick presentation design

- PowerPoint Animation Player for ActiveX allows work to be published as a Web page with animation and narration on the Internet

- "Pack and Go" feature quickly assembles and compresses presentations and support documents for efficient transportation

A significant feature of the PowerPoint application is the PowerPoint Viewer. This feature enables PowerPoint users to share their presentations with people who do not have PowerPoint installed on their computers. You can use the PowerPoint Viewer to view and print PowerPoint presentations exactly as they appear in PowerPoint. With the viewer, you can see all animation, graphics effects, action settings, hyperlinks, and custom shows.

PowerPoint also has the ability to create presentations that can be distributed on the World Wide Web, or to a company intranet. Presentations can be designed specifically for this purpose or can be taken from an existing presentation. These presentations can be converted to the Hypertext Markup Language (HTML) format so that they can be viewed by Web browsers. This type of expandability creates additional value in the presentation software arena, expanding the end user arena.

Multimedia Presentation/Authoring: mPower

Software Category: Multimedia Presentation/
Authoring
Platform(s): Macintosh and Windows
Company: Multimedia Design Corporation

mPower is an innovative product that is part authoring and part presentation software. Since the two are so closely connected, they are combined in this software so your presentation can become what you want it to be. If you want to develop a simple slide presentation, mPower lets you do so with very little knowledge or hands-on experience with the product. It works with a familiar slide metaphor and relies on a simple push-button interface. These features are beneficial to the occasional user. The on-screen menus and options are very simple, eliminating the confusion of finding an answer once a decision is in the project development phase. This interface and ease of use is what makes mPower redefine the word intuitive.

For those who want to take it farther, mPower provides an impressive array of features and connectivity that

Figure 5.3 mPower, from Multimedia Design Corporation, allows you to assign hot buttons over specific graphics to cause an action to happen when selected.

will suit a high-end, professional approach. mPower has the built-in capabilities to create QuickTime movies, capture still images, and digitize audio from CDs or microphones. It also has the capability to control CD players, laserdisc players, and other external devices without digitizing the sound or video first.

For interactive control, mPower allows the creation of hot buttons that can branch to other slides, play audio/video content, or even launch another application program (see Figure 5.3).

Software File Preparation

An important task in producing a multimedia presentation is the preparation of all of the files that will go into the production. This phase is somewhat similar to file preparation in a page layout program. In a page layout

Figure 5.4 The mPower screen allows various slides to be developed with the ability to incorporate various media elements.

program, such as Adobe PageMaker, elements that are a part of a document are prepared in other applications. For instance, type may be done in a word processing program, photographs are scanned or captured from a digital camera, line art may be produced in an illustration program, and original art may be produced from a paint program. Once these files are prepared and saved in a compatible format, they are ready to be placed into the page layout program. Once the files are imported they are placed in position on the page based on the designer's preference.

This scenario is similar to the preparation of files that will be used in a multimedia environment. Some of the file types are exactly the same as mentioned above, while others have additional functions. For instance, a multimedia presentation will contain backgrounds, type, photographs, illustrations, and other file types mentioned above. They will also contain files like sounds, animation, movies, music, computer graphics, and much more. All of these files must be saved in the proper format for importation into the authoring environment. Often times just saving the file in the proper format is not enough. With multimedia, issues like color look-up tables, sound quality, resolution, and other factors should be considered.

Modern-day Software Shopping

In the past, software was usually purchased through your local computer retailer. While at the store, you could obtain professional assistance and advice as to which software worked with which hardware and other pertinent information relative to the program. Originally, the computer retailer was the only place to buy software products. Not long after the desktop computer revolution began, specialty software stores began to open everywhere. Next, mail-order companies began to get into the act by offering a wide variety of titles for all areas of interest. This type of software distribution has really become popular due to the fact that the consumer is more computer and application savvy than ever before. Another reason that mail order is so popular is that you can usually order a product one evening and have it delivered to your doorstep the next morning.

Test-driving Software

There are several sources that offer software that can be taken on a "test-drive" without purchasing the product. There are options, such as downloading demos through the Internet, which allow you to try software programs. This concept is fantastic because many software applications look good on the spec sheet but may not meet your expectations as a real product. By trying it before you buy it, you know that you are purchasing exactly what you want, and know in advance that it will do what you want it to do.

The great feature of test-drive CD-ROMS is that the full working version of the software is often on the CD as well as a demo of the application. Of course, you do not automatically have access to the real software without paying the price. Here is how it works: Usually, the CD-ROM is free. When you receive the disk, you get instructions on operating the program as well as an 800 number. By calling the 800 number, you can provide a credit card number in exchange for a code that will allow you to instantly download the actual software you wish to purchase. The software usually contains an electronic manual or documentation.

The CD-ROM

In the old days, when software was distributed exclusively on floppy disks, the only product that came on the disk was the application program and perhaps some demo files or tutorials that illustrated how a project should look in that application. Early programs were small, their files were small, and their RAM requirements were small.

The 1990s have ushered in an era of more power, more storage, bigger monitors, and faster processing speed. As a result storage requirements have grown in direct proportion. The first Mac came with 128k RAM and no hard disk drive. The disk drive was a single sided, 400k unit. Optional external 400k drives were available, and were priced in the $500 range. Today there are many media-storage options such as the CD-ROM. As with technology-based products, the CD-ROM dropped in price during the 1990s and distribution to the masses became extremely practical. With the cost of mastering a CD-ROM dropping to approximately $1 each, software product distribution began to be commonplace in this medium.

The real demand for more space for application programs and support files happened gradually over a period of years. As software developers continued to upgrade, their products experienced growth in the amount of disk space and RAM required. Naturally, competition demanded that products contain all of the latest features and what the competitors were putting in their product. As these products grew in size, the distribution methods began to change. First, the software was shipped on numerous floppy disks. Next, they were shipped on numerous disks and the data files were compacted using a compression program. After a while, it became quite a project to purchase new software and load floppy after floppy into your Mac while the installer program decompressed and rejoined all the segments.

With the advent of the CD-ROM, a new avenue of data storage and distribution was born. CD-ROM technology introduced the capability to store the equivalent of hundreds of floppy disks on a single cd. A typical CD-ROM has a 650 MB capacity. This means that on one CD-ROM, you can place the equivalent of approximately 600 floppy disks. Does this mean the typical application program distributed on this media fills an entire CD-ROM? Not necessarily! A CD-ROM application, such as an encyclopedia or multimedia production, certainly could fill the entire disk, or more. However, most software applications will not even come close to filling 650 MB of space. What then is the importance of distributing software on CD-ROM? Here are several answers:

1. Cost is usually about $1.

2. Software companies can include support files, tutorials, and other information which add great value to the customer.

3. CD-ROM eliminates the need to swap disks.

4. All information is contained on one disk in most situations.

5. Trial versions of other software can be added.

Many CD-ROM software products come with trial versions of other software titles. Adobe Systems is a great example of a company who practices this. If you were to purchase, for example, Adobe Premiere, it would be shipped with a CD-ROM containing a full-working version of Premiere, support files, and trial versions of other Adobe products such as Photoshop, Illustrator, Dimensions, and Streamline. These trial versions usually consist of fully functional copies of the application, with the exception that you cannot save your work. This concept will allow the user

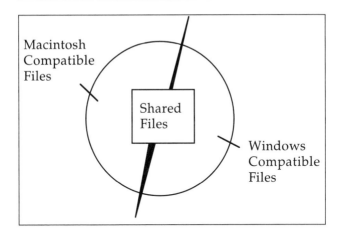

Figure 5.5 Macintosh- and Windows-compatible applications can be stored on the same CD-ROM. They can even share common data files.

to try the software, and see if it meets his needs before he buys it.

Numerous technical books are being authored that include CD-ROMS with tutorials and these trial versions of software programs that are applicable to the subject matter in the book. The good thing about these titles is that the consumer will be exposed to a variety of software applications by using these trial versions. As you shop for these books, the content of the CD-ROM is usually listed on the back of the book. If you are interested in trying out a program that may be included on the CD-ROM included with the book, it will make the purchase price of the book a better value.

You will find that many software developers are creating hybrid CD-ROM titles. This means that the disk contains both Macintosh- and Windows-compatible versions of the same presentation. The cd is mastered in a way that allows the user to simply insert the disk into his CD-ROM drive and boot the proper version. A software driver is present that recognizes what to do when placed in either computer. If you are a Macintosh user, typically, the Windows files are transparent. They are merely stored on the same media. This is true for Windows users; the Macintosh files are transparent. This format is becoming very commonplace with the convergence of platform technologies changing on a daily basis.

Chapter Six

Peripherals

Figure 6.1
Connectivity
to external
peripheral
devices is what
makes your
computer
versatile.

In the early days of desktop computing, the only items connected to the computer were the printer and perhaps a modem. Today there are numerous external devices that perform a variety of functions once connected. A computer peripheral is a device that connects to a personal computer to increase system functioning. These peripherals include digital cameras, microphones, scanners, laserdisc players, speakers, cd-recorders, hard disk drives, video cameras, and VCRs.

All of the "toys" that are a part of multimedia are quite intriguing. There are so many devices that interface with the computer that it is difficult to keep up with which does what and why! In technology-based environments, these products are constantly changing and growing in number. Knowing the products that can assist you best is important.

Probably the best way to keep up with new products and services is to subscribe to a trade publication that addresses issues surrounding your particular computer system. These publications provide fresh articles and reviews on the latest products and trends in this chang-

Figure 6.2 Multimedia computing requires numerous peripheral devices.

ing marketplace. These publications also cover specific computer and peripheral devices when they are introduced and let you know how the products perform. Subscribing to a publication that is user friendly is a good investment.

You do not have to be an expert to know what is going on in the computer peripheral market. Once you become involved in multimedia computing and are familiar with all of the componentry you will constantly be on the lookout for the latest and greatest device to assist your project. One thing you can always count on in this area is by the time you finally decide that the product is something you must have and get budget approval to make the purchase the price will drop. This is a typical scenario with technology-based equipment.

Approximately every six months you will see major shifts in product introductions and pricing strategies. If you haven't experienced this yet, you soon will. It is all a part of a game that manufacturers play that is somewhat dictated by the consumer. As consumers, we are always looking for the next level of product or service. Manufacturers cater to us by constantly offering upgrades. In the arena of computer peripherals, the next level is always where we want to be. There are so many products that allow us to elevate the performance and capabilities of our core computer system. Most of us will never satisfy our hunger for new products and capabilities.

Necessary Peripherals

There are some components that are mandatory to the multimedia computing process. These items include but are not limited to monitors, keyboards, disk drives, and printers. Other additions allow you to make your system perform and function according to what your job or work style demands. For instance, if you are involved in desktop publishing, you need a large monitor to display a two-page spread, a large hard drive to store color graphic scans, and a high-resolution printer or image setter for high-quality image output. These are some of the basics for this environment.

For multimedia production, your needs will vary. Although helpful, a large monitor may not be required. Most multimedia presentations are designed to be played on a 14-inch monitor. You may find that you will need a large capacity hard disk drive or a disk array for storing large files and for retrieving movies and sound files. A disk array is a series of hard drives that can transfer large amounts of information almost instantaneously. With multimedia production you may also need devices like VCRs, camcorders, CD-ROM recorders, microphones, and video digitizing cards.

With most peripheral devices, you will find that the same type of product is manufactured by a variety of vendors. These products are usually offered in a variety of price ranges. If you need to purchase a product and are unfamiliar with a vendor's reputation, you need to do your homework before you make your purchase. If you have searched for solutions on your own and are still confused, you need to consult a professional for further input. These professionals can be located by contacting computer retail stores, computer consultants, multimedia service bureaus, professional organizations, or users' associations.

When you are seeking this advice, make sure you have a relationship with these sources and that you trust their judgment and recommendations. Ask questions and take notes because there is much to learn. Another source for great advice is to consult with other professionals that are willing to share information. These users can provide excellent input because they have already gone through the selection process. Users' groups are also a great source of information. There are many users' groups that support different types of computer-related functions. Check in your area for computer or multimedia users' groups. If you do not know where to start, call a local computer retail store for advice.

Multimedia Support Products

Graphics, photographs, text, animation, and video— each of these elements has a source of origin. Each source of origin has its unique product and methods of development. When considering products for producing these images, you have to consider what your final production will be. Proper consideration for these products will include wise purchasing and appropriate training for each. This will ensure that as you compile all of your elements into a single multimedia production and utilize a smartly crafted script your production will come alive.

Figure 6.3 Digital cameras are the wave of the future—but are available now.

Input Device

You have several ways to input information with a computer. In word processing, you can either type your information in word for word or you may choose to scan in a typed document, using optical character recognition (OCR). This allows you to enter text in a short period of time. With multimedia, many types of information are used to prepare your project. For a fully customized production, you will use tools to capture images and information to your liking. To do this, you must consider several input devices to assist with your production. These include the following:

Digital Camera

With digital image capture technology, your photographs can be copied directly onto disk then into your computer for incorporation into your productions. There are many models of cameras available today ranging widely in quality and price. Digital cameras are designed to store a specific number of digital images. These devices offer instant image capture and are perfect for projects demanding a quick turnaround.

Video Camera

Your choice of a video camera for use in your multimedia productions will be based on what type of productions

Figure 6.4 Video cameras are an essential tool in multimedia computing.

you will be doing, what your final product will be, and who your audience is. For low- to medium-end productions, a high-quality consumer level video camera will suit your needs. If your plans are to go to the mass market with a commercial product, you will need the best quality original video product you can produce. Digital cameras are an excellent solution; however, if you are on a strict budget, this technology may be an expensive alternative. Make a purchasing decision based on your immediate as well as anticipated needs.

Videotape Unit

Like the video camera, VCRs come in various price ranges, qualities, and formats. These formats include VHS, S-VHS, 8mm, and Hi-8. There are no digital VCRs that offer professional results. For average multimedia usage S-VHS and Hi-8 offer exceptional results. There are also video decks that can be controlled by your computer. The quality of your equipment should be determined in part by the quality of your final product. When placing video footage into your computer for editing, your video images can be enhanced with various software effects. Sometimes, you can compensate problems in your videotape by using these software techniques.

Figure 6.5 A sound file as displayed on the computer.

Sound Input Devices

Have you ever pressed the "mute" button on your TV remote control and just watched the screen with no sound? Images are good, but moving images without sound are not as effective as combining the two. Sound, whether narration, sound effects, or music, is vital to the full implementation of a multimedia production.

There are several ways to get sound into your computer. Many computers come with a hand-held microphone for voice annotation or recording. Sound can also be obtained through clip resources, like clip art. These files can range from effect sounds to music clips that are especially prepared for the computer and multimedia productions.

Sound can also be created by connecting musical instruments to your computer. This process is called Musical Instrument Digital Interface (MIDI). This format converts the sound into a digital signal. Being digital means that the sound file will be clear, equal to cd audio quality, and ready for instant playback, at specified locations in your production.

Figure 6.6 A typical flatbed desktop scanner.

Scanner

There are enough scanners on the market today to really confuse a potential buyer. Before purchasing a scanner, it is imperative that you do your homework. Following are some questions you should consider in a scanner purchase.

- Does it have a color preview feature?

- Does the scanner save images to RAM or disk? Scanning to RAM is a faster process. If you have a low amount of RAM your file will be saved to disk. This is slower, but nonetheless a workable solution.

- At what resolution does the scanner capture information? The higher the dots per inch (dpi), the better the image will be.

- If software is bundled with the scanner, is it something you will use and is it a good value as a bundled package?

If color fidelity is vital to your work, buy the best scanner you can. Some manufacturers have a better reputation with optics and color systems than others. For serious media work, a hand-held scanner is not really a viable option. You may also want to consider the Optical Character Recognition (OCR) capabilities of the scanner. This probably has nothing to do with multimedia but as long as you are buying a scanner, see if it has the capability. Many desktop scanners bundle OCR software with the scanner.

Hard Drive/External Storage Devices

When you first began computing, you may have started with a word processing program. As you know, you can get a lot of documents on a single floppy disk. This is not true with multimedia computing. Digital photographs consume a great deal of disk space. Moving pictures with sound, animation, special effects, and numerous support files require even more space. Not only is more space required but speed becomes an important consideration. High-capacity drives, 1 gigabyte or more, usually offer fast access times and transfer rates. This performance is necessary for multimedia computing. You will have to pay more for drives with more capacity and faster access times, but it is worth it. There are also special drives designed to handle the demands of transferring the enormous amount of information associated with multimedia. These are called audio/video (AV) drives. They are constructed to handle the rapid retrieval and display of full-motion video and audio, which can be around 1MB of information per second.

A Review of Media Storage Devices

Laserdisc

Laserdiscs are to video what CD is to audio. With the CD, the audio quality is superior to audiotape. With a laserdisc, the video and audio quality are superior to videotape. Videodisks are used in many kiosk applications that require large amounts of data demanding superior image quality. Another advantage of videodisk is that the access time to a particular segment on the disk is very fast. For other multimedia applications, certain laserdisc units offer the ability to be controlled by your computer. If this is a consideration in your multimedia future, purchase wisely and make sure that this capability is a part of the unit.

Media	Size	Capacity
Floppy Disk	800k	200 typewritten pages
Floppy Disk	1.4MB	300 typewritten pages
Hard Disk	20MB	5,000 typewritten pages
Hard Disk	40MB	10,000 typewritten pages
Hard Disk	100MB	25,000 typewritten pages
Hard Disk	1 Gigabyte	250,000 typewritten pages

Table 6.1 Storage capacities of various media types.

CD-ROM *Recorder*

The CD-ROM has become a mainstream product. Having the ability to read them is a requirement, and having the ability to make them is becoming more and more popular. As a multimedia producer, you will eventually find the CD-ROM recorder essential.

A CD-ROM recorder allows you to record CD-ROMS. These recordable discs cost anywhere from around four dollars to thirty dollars based on the quality and source. This format is excellent for copying multimedia presentations because of their large capacity. Each disk can hold up to 650 MB. They are durable, inexpensive, and have a very long shelf life.

Figure 6.7 CD-ROM recording device.

One of the differences between recording to a CD-ROM and recording to a hard disk drive or other format is that once you record, or burn, a CD-ROM, the information is permanently recorded. If you want to modify the disk in any way you simply must start over. This is not a major concern, just the process that you have to get used to. An exception to this is the compact disc re-writable (CD-RW). This works just like the CD-R, but allows re-writing over existing content, much like floppies, ZIPs, and other magnetic media.

With the advent of the newer Digital Versatile Disk (DVD), this process will be similar. The exception is that the DVD will hold much more information than the traditional CD-ROM.

Part II

Media Preparation

Chapter Seven

Developing Your
Graphic Images

The creation of graphic images for multimedia is critically important, due to the fact that in any multimedia production, there are a variety of images. These images can be static, animated, or full motion. Remember that a picture is worth a thousand words; therefore, each graphic element should be the best it can be in content and quality. These images may be in the form of a photograph, interactive button, a computer illustration, or video footage from your camcorder.

The good thing about working on a computer and developing computerized graphic images is that your work can be saved and modified to easily create variations. All of this is done without having to recreate the product from scratch. If you have ever worked with pen and ink, watercolor, oil paint, or other medium, you know that once the project is completed, it is final. To modify the piece would require recreating, touching up, or even starting from scratch.

Traditional art forms can be recreated in digital format for use on your computer. Microsoft offers a variety of classic art pieces on CD-ROM that can be viewed on your computer screen. Not only are the classics available in this technology, but you too can have your creations in digital format for manipulation or viewing on your computer system.

By utilizing digital cameras, scanners, and other input devices, any art form can be captured and turned into a computer graphic. These images in digital format can be used for a variety of purposes. They can also be enhanced and reworked to form entirely new creations as illustrated

Figure 7.1 An original piece of art, scanned into the computer and transformed into a new art form for use as a logo.

in Figure 7.1. You can even capture screen images and use them in your productions.

Figure 7.2 is a screen shot from Travelrama, USA, from Sanctuary Woods. This screen demonstrates several multimedia screen elements. Of course, each production will vary in the type of graphic as well as the quantity. Remember that this is an art form, and implementation of techniques and style will vary with each project.

Producing the Art Form Needed for the Project

Backgrounds

Any presentation you are involved with will contain a background. Most of us prefer to have some creative control over what the background will look like. Most presentation and authoring software programs contain a variety of predesigned backgrounds.

Multimedia projects are very much like works of art. Each one will have a different style, color palette, and feel. What makes these projects unique is the content and the creative direction given to the creator. Unique background selections can truly provide individualism and character to any project.

Solids are the old standby. Textures can add a different feel to a presentation, and often are available to support various themes such as nautical, outdoor, weather, etc. There are a wide selection of textures that can be obtained through existing clip-art sources (see Figure 7.3).

Figure 7.2 A screen from *Travelrama, USA,* from Sanctuary Woods. This screen demonstrates many of the elements that must be designed or procured for production. Some of the elements include: Photography, line art, scanned images, buttons, text, and original computer graphics.

Solid   **Texture**   **Photograph**

Figure 7.3 Backgrounds used in multimedia productions can be almost anything.

Figure 7.4 Any piece of art can be made into a button. They are as customizable as that artist wants them to be.

Figure 7.5 Buttons can be very spartan in design. These buttons are straightforward, making their function simple and direct.

Photographs can offer specific content and theme development, creating a very focused enhancement to any presentation. The variety of historical, thematic, and contemporary topics, currently available on CD-ROM, are virtually endless. This, combined with the ability to capture your own images, will provide total control of graphic production for background materials.

Buttons

One thing you typically see on the screen of an interactive presentation is the presence of some form of button. Traditionally, to respond to an interactive CD-ROM or other form of presentation, you must click a button. Buttons are used to start, stop, go forward or reverse, return, play, or to perform various other forms of interactive control. For the

Figure 7.6 Some screens contain buttons that are activated upon a click or touch. In this example, objects come to life with sound and animation.

most part, buttons are just a small representation of what we are used to in real life (see Figures 7.4 and 7.5).

Often, however, what functions as a button is not our traditional vision of what a button should look like. Figure 7.6 demonstrates a creative use of interactivity. The demo suggests that the user click one of the labeled keys on the keyboard. By clicking on one of these keys, an action will occur in response to what the key has been programmed to do. An example of this would be that when a key is selected, you will go to another screen, or begin a sound-track, or animated sequence.

In this example, a specific graphic area is assigned to function as the button. This is identical to the selection of a rectangular or round button, with the exception that the selectable area conforms to the specific graphic, no matter what shape it is. The button will maintain its function no matter where it is selected.

Figure 7.7 In this example, a
graphic functions as a button.

Figure 7.8
A predesigned button set from
Instant Buttons & Controls,
from Stat Media.

Buttons can be created in a variety of software applications. Vectorized drawing programs, such as Adobe Illustrator, Macromedia FreeHand, or other drawing programs,
work fine. Bitmapped programs such as Adobe Photoshop
also offer a design option. Figure 7.7 is an example of a
bitmapped button.

An alternative to creating your own buttons is to let
someone do it for you. There are companies that specialize
in the development of such products. Stat Media, Inc., creates a program called Instant Buttons & Controls. This
product contains over 1,000 buttons and controls (see Figure 7.8). These predesigned elements are not only graphic
files, but also contain code to control interactivity when
used with Macromedia Director. They can be copied and
pasted into a Director production and are ready for
instant use.

Figure 7.9 Lineart graphics can be used for signage or a variety of graphics. Vectorized art, from programs like Adobe Illustrator and Macromedia FreeHand, allow you great creative freedom and easy control of lineart.

Logos/Line Art

Logos and line art files can be created in a variety of methods. Logos, like Figure 7.9, could be created in a drawing program, like Adobe Illustrator or Macromedia FreeHand. Once the art is prepared, it can be turned into a bitmapped image for placement or integration into a specific art file or can become a part of a composite image. Often times, if a particular font is not available to produce the desired image, it can be drawn and can be an art file.

Producing a graphic this way is very practical. The image may be difficult to manipulate as a bitmapped graphic, but easily modified if saved as a vector graphic. Remember that vector graphics can be saved and exported from Illustrator or FreeHand into paint programs such as Photoshop.

There are also numerous clip-art sources to obtain lineart files. These electronic files can be manipulated to reflect the desired effect you are after. After a period of working between vector and bitmapped graphics, you can learn what works best for various situations.

Remember that lineart can be placed directly into a multimedia production. Sometimes it will function better as a bitmap image.

Photography

Photography has been around for well over a century and, in this high-tech world, the photograph is still the driving force in graphic communication. A benefit of photography is that it is accessible to everyone (see Figure 7.10). Of course, there are varying degrees of quality in both cameras and processing, as well as with the photographer, but photography is everywhere. Since photography has been around so long, there are plenty of existing images that can be integrated into a multimedia presentation. By using a scanner, these images can have new life as electronic media. Through the use of digital cameras, images can be shot and captured by the computer almost instantly.

The application and growth of products and services in this area has grown tremendously in the past few years. This is evidenced by the number of stock photography services that are available in both printed and digital photography. There are even photo services available on the Internet that allow you to subscribe, browse a photo library, then download images on demand.

PhotoCD

A big technology break in the past few years is the introduction of the PhotoCD. This technology allows you to take your 35mm film to a photo lab and have your photos converted into digital files on a CD. Once converted, you can insert the CD into your computer's CD-ROM drive and have access to your photographs as digital graphic files. The images are typically stored in five different resolutions. For screen display, you use a lower resolution image. For a printed product, you use a higher resolution image for the best print quality.

Figure 7.10 Photography is accessible to everyone.

This product, originally introduced as a consumer-level product with commercial overtones, is proving to be an extremely viable technology. Though the consumer applications have not been a boon to the industry, graphic artists and multimedia users are finding this to be a product with many avenues of usage.

As more and more options are opening up to enhance computer imaging and multimedia production, presentations are becoming increasingly larger, requiring more storage space and heftier hardware and processing speed. Images used in multimedia projects must be of excellent quality and oftentimes large enough to be used as a background. Images stored on PhotoCDs provide excellent quality, and CDs can store around 100 images.

The PhotoCD process allows you to have your film processed onto a CD rather than to traditional printed photos. This process is extremely useful in the realm of multimedia. One of the advantages is that it allows the user to work with a pure image at a choice of resolutions. The image is processed digitally onto the CD, giving a perfect image over and over again. No additional scanning or capturing is required. It also serves as an excellent archival device.

Consideration should be given to resolutions based on what your use of the product will be. If you plan to go to print with your image, then you may consider the Pro PhotoCD format. However, if your application for the images is strictly on-screen multimedia production or presentation, then lower resolutions will work just fine. Remember that the typical monitor used in a multimedia application will not display all of the information that is contained in a high-resolution image such as 4,096 by 6,144. Be aware also that with higher resolution graphics, more disk space will be required.

PhotoCDs capture your film onto the CD in five resolutions, the highest being 2,048 by 3,072. There is also a professional level PhotoCD. This is called the Pro PhotoCD. This format allows a total of six resolutions with the highest at 4,096 by 6,144 (See Table 7.1).

Stock Photography on PhotoCD

Utilizing stock photography is a great way to enhance or develop a presentation in a timesaving and economical

Resolution	Usage
192 x 128	Thumbnails
384 x 256	General Purpose
768 x 512	Monitor Display
1536 x 1024	TV Output
3072 x 2048	Printing

Table 7.1 PhotoCD resolutions and their applications.

manner. You can instantly capture photos, movies, animation, and other graphic file types in a tremendous time and cost saving process. Companies such as Image Club Graphics offer a PhotoCD product line that features numerous photos on a variety of subject matter such as space, business, industry, textures, backgrounds, and lifestyles. These PhotoCDs contain a browser file that allows you to view the contents without requiring additional software applications. As with all PhotoCDs, these digital images come in five resolutions. These photographs are compiled by well known photographers and are high quality. Use for this medium includes newsletters, multimedia presentations, brochures, ads, and more.

Using PhotoCD technology is an excellent way to save time and money in the preparation of images for multimedia production. Much time can be saved over the traditional process of taking photographs, having them processed and then scanning. Consideration must be given, however, to the fact that PhotoCDs are not a one-hour, instant processing situation. Many processing labs have this work sent out for production. Make sure that proper planning and time is allowed.

Video Capture

You can record video images and sound directly to your computer using one of several movie capture software applications currently on the market. These applications are quickly becoming very sophisticated. To record video into an application such as Adobe Premiere you need a video digitizing card with video digitizing component software which is supplied by the manufacturer of the digitizer card. If you want to record sound as well as images, you need a computer with a sound input port or a sound digitizing device with input software.

Acquiring video images/footage from a VCR, camcorder or laserdisc unit into your computer requires a large amount of hard disk space and sufficient amount of RAM.

Also required is a video capture board and a software program that is capable of "grabbing" the video frames that you want to save as a digital movie on your computer. After you have acquired the video files, you will also need software that allows you to edit the movie.

Another tremendous advantage of capturing video on your computer is the fact that this video is made up of numerous still pictures. Based on the resolution and quality of these images, individual frames can be selected for use as a static graphic. If the quality level is not good enough for your use, these images can be great for FPO (for position only) shots for storyboarding scenes for a production. See Chapter 9 for more information about capturing video.

Computer Graphics

Computer graphics can be developed in a variety of ways. A computer graphic can be a simple lineart drawing or a scanned photograph (see Figure7.11). It can be an illustration created in a three-dimensional drawing program, or an image compiled from a variety of original sources. Once an image enters the computer it becomes a computer art form. Once repurposed, it becomes a product of digital technology.

All images used in a multimedia production will become computer graphics no matter if they are created, captured, scanned, or created by clip art. What makes computer-based multimedia production so attractive and feasible, is the fact that the computer is the logical device to capture, manipulate, and integrate all of these elements into a cohesive product or production.

In multimedia, any image can become a suitable graphic for on-screen display. Authoring programs like Director accept a wide variety of file formats making it easy to incorporate images into a production.

Figure 7.11 Computer graphics can be just about anything. The biker watch shown here was scanned, then traced, then filled with gradients. This was a three step process.

Type

Type, like graphics, can take on different forms in multimedia. A very important consideration when using type is that in many instances, the type that is seen on screen is actually a graphic image. If you are producing a presentation for use on your computer only, or for an in-house function, then all the support elements that you utilize are built into your computer, ensuring that screen displays of graphics and type are workable. However, if you are producing a product that will be sent to others you must make sure that what you distribute will work on other machines. In order for your presentation to display correctly on other computers, those systems must contain the same type style. If they do not, the type may be substituted with a different typeface causing an undesirable or unreadable visual effect on their screen.

How do you work around the previously mentioned scenario? One way is to ensure that the user has that particular font on his system. Another way is to send a copy of the font with your production and have the user install that font in his computer. However, fonts are a copyrighted software product. An alternative is to use public domain typefaces and avoid licensing and copyright infringements.

What works best is to make your typeface a part of the screen image. If the type is to be constantly displayed on the screen, for example as a part of the background, then it can be just that. If the text is to appear randomly, then it can be a smaller graphic, being introduced to the presentation as needed. The real benefit of having your text as a graphic is that it is not subject to dependence on a specific type family being present on the computer in order for it to display well on the screen.

Creation

When you cannot find a piece of art that suits your needs for a particular project, what do you do? You create it yourself. Today, there are plenty of sophisticated drawing programs that will allow you to design anything you can imagine. Programs like Adobe Photoshop, Adobe Illustrator, Macromedia FreeHand, and Fractal Design Painter allow amazing productions from your desktop computer.

Creating art that is acceptable for a particular project is totally up to the artist. One real advantage of creating electronic art is the fact that you can borrow from other images or sources to create an original art form. For instance, you may want to use a part of a scan that you have captured as the base for a new creation. Once this image is in your computer, you can enhance it and give it a new appearance. You could also merge a piece of clip art into your production to add further enhancements.

Chapter Eight

Sound

Hi-fi, stereo, split channel, digital audio, CD-ROM-quality. These are some of the terms relative to sound that we have become accustomed to in this sophisticated, technological age. We forget that in the early days of radio any type of sound at all was good enough. When television came along it too had sound. That was also good enough. Volume adjustment was great but tone adjustment was even better. Just as most technology improves with time, so does sound, especially in the products and processes that make it happen. Determining what is "good enough" sound has changed.

Sound Technology

There have been some significant breakthroughs in sound quality over the years. Great strides have been made not only in the area of delivery, but also in the method in which sound is produced, transmitted, and even stored.

From a consumer standpoint, High-Fidelity, or hi-fi, sound was a major innovation. Stereo sound truly added a new dimension to a presentation, allowing sounds to be split and become more lifelike. In the 1970s, quadraphonic sound was added to the existing stereo systems allowing sound to come from four sources. This was supposed to be the rave, but never caught on. The quadraphonic format died almost overnight.

Figure 8.1 The technology contrast between vinyl LPs and CD-roms.

The next major sensation in sound was the advent of compact disk technology. This innovation set new standards for sound clarity and delivery. The CD-ROM format allows sound to be recorded to and stored in metal pits on a 5-inch plastic disk in a digital format. Storing sound or music in a digital format means that the sound information is converted from a continuous flow of sound, or an analog format, to numbers. These numbers are ones and zeros, which turn on and off as they are read by the laser in the CD-ROM player. This digital information is then processed and amplified, providing excellent sound quality with little or no distortion. With the advent of digital recording, sound can be reproduced consistently, over and over again, with the last copy sounding as good as the first.

Digital recording technology is quite different from the way a record player worked. Each time the needle was placed in a groove on the vinyl record, the quality of the sound diminished a bit due to the direct contact. Even though the LP is still around the CD-ROM format is the dominant distribution medium of choice for audio.With CD-ROM technology, information is stored in small metal pits and read by a laser. Therefore, the disk is never touched giving a long life span to the disk format (see Figure 8.1).

Next to visual images, sound is the most important part of multimedia. Properly executed sound files can communicate exactly what you want to say when you want to

Figure 8.2 The CD is the preferred distribution medium for high-quality sound reproduction.

say it. This is critical when you are trying to communicate the same message to the masses. Proper sound editing, concise wording, and well implemented timing is what makes sound so important in multimedia presentations.

Without question, multimedia productions have much more impact with the addition of sound. As with any type of visual presentation, sound provides a dimension that assists in clear communication and provides gripping emotional impact. Consider watching the evening news with the volume turned off. Think about watching a cartoon without all of those crazy sound effects, or how about watching a sci-fi space epic without the spectacular sound effects that we all enjoy. These just would not be the same.

As you view a multimedia presentation that possesses excellent sound quality, you receive the benefits of a more dynamic experience. As with good visuals, good sound can drastically enhance any production.

Sound Types in Multimedia

Types of sound typically required in various areas of multimedia development and presentation consist of the following.

Narration is a voice recording for specific use at a predetermined time or "on demand" in an interactive environment. Narration says what you want to say, and by using multimedia technologies, when you want to say it. If demonstrating a process or procedure, it can be repeated, on demand, at the user's discretion.

Sound effect is a particular sound used for impact during a slide transition, animated sequence, or in conjunction with a special visual effect. In Computer-Based Training (CBT), sound effects can be extremely useful by providing a positive or negative response.

Music is used for background sound, to create mood, to demonstrate specific music tracks as a point of interest or sale, and to set the pace of a presentation.

Each of these elements can work independently, or can be used in combination to meet specific production criteria.

Obtaining Sound

Obtaining narration, sound effects, and music for inclusion in multimedia projects can be simple or complicated. This process is based upon two things: what you are trying to obtain and your level of understanding of the resources needed to acquire them.

The next section will review how each sound source is obtained.

Narration

Narration for multimedia projects is usually information specific to your presentation or message. Therefore, the information must be created specifically for each production. The developer creates the narrative sound track himself or has it done by an outside source. Some of the considerations are:

- Can I do it myself?
- Is my voice quality sufficient for the job?
- Do I have the equipment to do the recording?
- If I use an outside source, where do I go?
- Does my project have the funds to pay for outside sources?

Of course, each project will have its own set of demands and constraints; therefore, be prepared to do what it takes to make it happen.

Figure 8.3 Capturing voice recording directly into the computer.

Some presentation scenarios will require you to provide narration as graphics are displayed on a screen. If you are developing an interactive project designed for mass distribution, a decision must be made as to how to do it. For professional quality narration, time and money are almost always considerations. Careful preplanning and experimentation will guide you through the process. Experience is an excellent teacher, providing real-world knowledge as to what works best. Also, do not forget to seek the wisdom of those who have gone down the road before you. Stay ahead of the game by learning from their successes and failures.

Another method is to use a microphone, perhaps the one that came with your computer, as an input source. Many computers come with sound recording capability built in. More recent Macintosh models and MPCs have this feature. Some multimedia monitors have microphones and speakers built into them. This will work for starters. One way to get voice recording into the computer is to take a recording, from an audiotape or other source, and connect the device to an audio (or audio/video) board in the computer and capture the sound track into a program designed to convert the file to digital information.

To simply record a sound, for example for a voice annotation, a control panel is available that allows the recording process to happen. Figure 8.3, taken from the Macintosh operating system, reflects the familiar controls that are

Figure 8.4 Computer systems with sound capture capabilities provide options for sound source.

universal for record, stop, pause, and play. These buttons are similar to VCRs, laserdisc players, and CD-ROM audio players. By pressing the record button, you can record the voice or sound of your choice. Once saved, this file can be used for a variety of applications, such as for inclusion into a media presentation or as a system sound.

The aforementioned scenario represents the easiest, most direct method for capturing a sound into the computer. However, there are other methods that will add more sophistication to this process. For higher quality output the proper microphone, sound capture software, and knowledge of how to process the sound information is required.

Sound Effects

Sound effects are perhaps the most commonly used sound format in the development of multimedia productions. Properly used sound effects can be very effective at getting a point across and grabbing the attention of an audience. This type of audio file is also one of the easiest formats to obtain.

Typically, sound effects can be obtained from companies that specialize in producing sound effects for distribution. These effects are usually distributed on CD-ROM due to the size of the individual files, the number of sound files, and the format in which they are stored. A sound effects CD-ROM could include anywhere from 50 to 2,000 sound files, stored in a variety of formats. These formats include .aif, .wav, and others, and are compatible with Macintosh and Windows applications. These files can also be saved in a format that is compatible with specific sound recording software, such as Macromedia's SoundEdit 16. You can also expect to find an assortment of canned sound files with the purchase of sound editing software programs. Some multimedia authoring programs also offer a collection of sound effects as a part of their program.

Clip media sound files are typically prepared at a different sampling rate. That is, the lower the sampling rate, the smaller the file size. For example, simple sound effects, like a "boing" or "crash" will probably be saved at a low kilohertz (kHz), thus yielding a smaller file. On the other hand, a music file with high-quality stereo sound, will be made available in a choice of sizes, such as 22 or 44 kHz. This option will allow the user to determine the quality needed based on the impact needed or the storage space available.

Music

Like sound effects, music files can be obtained through various clip media vendors. There are music clips to support any musical taste and to accompany any style graphic or video.

Basic Sound

These days it seems as though computers are capable of managing and running almost anything. One element that the computer manages quite well is sound. Following is some information that will help you understand computerized sound.

Sound is typically an analog process. That is, sound is a continuous flow of sound information or sound waves. This is the method an audiotape employs to handle the sound recording process. The information on the tape plays in a sequence providing a continuous flow of information.

Figure 8.5 This screen is from SoundEdit 16, from Macromedia. This sound editing program lists sample sizes in kilohertz, or thousand of samples per second. CD quality audio is captured at an interval of approximately 1/44,100 second apart, as shown.

Computers manage and process digital information. Sounds created on the computer are digital from the beginning. When importing sounds into the computer, for example from an analog tape player, the computer must convert this information into a digital format. Once the file is converted, it can read the digital information and play it back with precision.

The process of converting analog sound into digital sound is called sampling. The computer captures many samples from the original sound source and converts the information into digits that a computer can read. Sampling sound rates will vary. For instance sampling can be done anywhere from 11 kHz to 44 kHz. These numbers, eleven or forty-four, represent the number of times that a sample is taken per second. Therefore, an 11 kHz sampling rate would be only one-fourth of the quality of a sample taken at 44 kHz . This also means that the size of the file created is proportional to the sampling rate used. The word Hertz means "per second," so 22 hertz would be 22 samples taken

Figure 8.6 Sound waves as they appear in a digital format utilizing Macromedia's SoundEdit 16.

per second. Kilo means "thousands," therefore 22 kilohertz would equal 22,000 samples per second.

Twenty-two kHz seems to be an average size for a sound file and is a typical sample rate for sound used in multimedia productions. The quality can be even better by sampling at 44 kHz, but based on your production requirements you may not need the higher quality sound. Sound, like other files, takes up disk space based on quality. Better quality sound equals a larger data file.

How sounds are used in multimedia productions will vary greatly. Like many other aspects of this technology, study closely and learn from successful titles currently on the market. Do not let the technicalities cloud your creative spirit.

Advanced Sound

A popular form of sound used in multimedia is called sampled sound or digital audio. Another format, Musical Instrument Digital Interface (MIDI), is a much more efficient and desirable way to deliver sound in a multimedia presentation.

There are numerous software programs dedicated to sound capture, playback, and modification. These programs allow this information to be converted to digital files that can be manipulated on the computer. Once the file is digital, it can be saved, stored, and played back in multiple formats.

If sounds had a look, the look would be similar to Figure 8.6. Like other types of computer files, this information

Figure 8.7
Some of the available sound effects used in editing digital sound files.

can be edited from its original form. Sound digitizing and editing programs, such as SoundEdit 16 allow you to edit the sound in many ways.

To add an effect, such as reverb for an echo, all you have to do is to add this effect to your original sound file. The list of special effects is large, giving you great access to creative sound effects. With most multimedia computer systems, the ability to capture sound is built into the unit in the form of a microphone. With older systems, the addition of a sound processing card will give you the ability to capture and edit sound files.

As with color graphic scans, sound files take up a considerable amount of disk space. Scans of course are based upon the physical size and the color depth to determine their size. Sound files grow larger in size the longer they are, and the higher level of quality in which they are recorded. As you develop a production, keep these factors in mind.

Figure 8.8 Sound is projected from the computer in a variety of ways, some yielding better results than others.

Sound Playback

Like other elements of multimedia preparation, sound deserves careful consideration as to the method and location that your presentation will be viewed. Most computers these days are equipped with at least a basic speaker system to handle voice and music. Those that do not, have at least a basic speaker built into the computer or the monitor. If the computer system is an MPC then sound hardware and software have been integrated into the system. This is usually done by allowing connections, through a video card or external sound connector, to a pair of external speakers. Based on the configuration, these speakers can be free-standing or can be mounted on the side of the monitor. In other scenarios, speakers are built directly into the monitor itself.

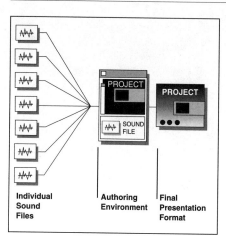

Figure 8.9
Individual sound files saved for playback as programmed or on demand.

Individual Sound Files | Authoring Environment | Final Presentation Format

Using Sound
Files Effectively in Productions

Like the many graphic files it takes to make a production, sound files can consist of many different files. If the production is narrated, the sound files will usually be a series of small narrations. These narrations, once interwoven into the production, will appear to be a part of a coherent message. In the authoring software environment, smaller files work better by being turned on and off as needed. The scripting portion of the authoring software will play the sound file at the appropriate time. The coordination of the sound file and the graphic is extremely important.

Some projects may be designed to provide continuous narration with background visuals and music. In situations like these, a continuous sound file, containing music as well as the narration, could be developed. A presentation of this type will become a large data file in just a short period of time. Keep this in mind if this method of delivery is chosen. This will impact the storage space required and will dictate from which type of device the presentation will be played.

Chapter Nine

Video

Multimedia, the integration of numerous elements, is enhancing presentation design like never before. Perhaps the most stimulating of all of the elements involved in multimedia is the integration of video. Various developers and companies are making video quality better and accessible to everyone, and we are enjoying the benefits of this exciting technology today. Why is video at the forefront of all the other media types? Perhaps it is due to the fact that we are visually oriented, and therefore relate to images that move.

We relate to what we see and are capable of interpreting messages visually, even without the addition of audio support. In our media-based society, especially through the venue of television programming, our visuals are not just pictures, they consist of composite graphic information. This includes full-motion photography combined with titles and graphics that are capable of telling us or selling us just about anything. When this is combined with audio, the medium becomes even more powerful.

In the realm of computer-based multimedia development and presentation, acquiring video into a personal computer is a relatively new capability. The fact that this technology exists is a technological marvel. Nonetheless, changes and capabilities in this arena continue to grow by leaps and bounds, and we can expect many changes in the future.

So, where do you begin to learn about how to capture video and integrate video into your computer? How is it handled in video editing software? How is it stored once converted into digital information? What are the Mac/PC issues? These, and other topics, will be addressed in this chapter.

QuickTime

A new form of video was introduced to the computer screen in 1991 through a revolutionary process called QuickTime by Apple Computer. QuickTime introduced the excitement of video to our personal computers, and ushered in yet another avenue in which we could use our computers. Before QuickTime there was text, graphics, sound, animation, and other basics that would allow development of a variety of media presentations. With the advent of QuickTime, the dimension of video was introduced, providing much greater depth and content-rich material to ordinary presentations.

QuickTime's revolutionary technology allows multiple images to be stored and played back at a speed that brings the image to life on the computer screen. QuickTime did for digital pictures what movie film did for movies. As you know, movie film is made up of many individual pictures

Analog

Digital

QuickTime

Figure 9.1 The videotape conversion from analog to digital.

that, when played back at the proper speed, appear to be lifelike. QuickTime controls the timing associated with many digital images, allowing them to appear in a movie format when played. Animation also works in this manner. Proper timing applied to the artwork or photograph yields a realistic presentation.

QuickTime was originally developed for the Macintosh, but the technology has since been expanded to allow Windows to use this format to play video files. With the advent of this technology, many software and hardware products have been introduced that assist in the capture, playback, and editing of video footage.

As we discussed in Chapter 8, sound files begin in an analog format. In order for these files to be used as computer files, they must be converted into a digital file format. Doing this allows the file to be saved and manipulated for future use. This same concept applies to video. Video captured, say from a camcorder, is analog information, or a continuous flow of information. It, like sound, must be converted into a digital file in order for it to be used and played back on the computer. Another comparison is the scanning process. When scanning a photograph on a flat bed scanner, you place the photo face down on the scanner. As it scans, a light passes over the picture capturing the image and converting it into a digital file. Once the image is converted into a digital format, it can be manipulated on the computer by a variety of painting or photo retouching software programs, or perhaps placed directly into a page layout or authoring program. Once videotape is converted into a digital file, it too can be manipulated in numerous ways through a variety of software applications.

In Figure 9.1, the illustration on top demonstrates how videotape stores magnetic signals, as analog signals. The second illustration shows the analog file converted to a digital format. The image on the bottom represents the digital file displayed on the computer screen in the form of a QuickTime Movie. The digital files appear as a series of individual pictures, which when played at the proper speed appear to be a movie.

Figure 9.2
QuickTime can accept these formats and play them back on Macintosh and Windows systems.

The QuickTime extension allows Macintosh and Windows users to integrate high-quality graphics, sounds, video, and animation into various documents. The QuickTime software includes utilities that allow you to play, edit, and create movies on the Macintosh, as well as save them in a format that will play on systems running Windows. Your projects can consist of video only, audio only, still images with sound, or a combination of options.

QuickTime movies are becoming a mainstay in desktop computing. Many applications, including word processing, databases, and authoring software, will accept QuickTime movie integration.

QuickTime is compatible with all Macintosh computers with the exception of the original 128k Macintosh. QuickTime movies are also compatible with Windows systems by adding the QuickTime for Windows extension. To use this extension you must have a hard disk and a minimum of 4MB of free memory. Refer to Figures 9.3, 9.4, and 9.5.

QuickTime Reference Movies

QuickTime reference movies contain no video or sound of their own, but rather have pointers or links to the original movie file. One advantage of this format is that new

WORKSHOP

Figure 9.3 A QuickTime movie can be various sizes. This example is 160 x 120 pixels.

Figure 9.4 A QuickTime movie can be a "sound only" movie. These sound files have all of the QuickTime features with the exception of no picture.

Figure 9.5 The QuickTime movie window control bar provides many of the features that your VCR may have.

movies can be made using parts from existing movies without modifying the contents of the original. This is helpful because it allows sharing of files, and conservation of storage space. If you choose to make these reference movies, it is important to remember that you must not rename the original movie or move it to another location, such as another folder on the hard drive. The movies and names must remain intact in order for these references to access the necessary files.

Disk access time, or the time it takes to read information from another movie and place it into a new movie, is affected by the proximity of all of the files that make up the movie. The optimum location for all files is the same folder, or directory, on your hard drive. A decrease in time will take place if the source information is spread out in other drives or buried in other directories or folders. Any changes done to a QuickTime reference movie must be done with careful planning. A domino effect will happen if any component is removed or renamed in the structure of the movie (see Figure 9.7).

If you plan to use a QuickTime reference movie that includes linking to a file that is located on a CD-ROM drive, and your drive is single-speed and perhaps an older model, your access time will decrease significantly when pulling information from a movie or sound file located on that drive. Once again, this is not an optimal environment for maximum performance. Consider this as you manage your files and presentations.

QuickTime for Macintosh and AVI for Windows

When we think of multimedia these days, we almost always think of video as a focal point. In desktop video creation, there are two major players. For the Macintosh Operating System, there is QuickTime, and as previously mentioned, QuickTime for Windows. For the Windows environment, there is also Video for Windows. Video for

Figure 9.6 QuickTime movies can be self-contained or can depend on other files in order to function properly. This decision is up to the user.

Figure 9.7 A QuickTime reference movie uses other video and sound files in order to play back the movie.

Figure 9.8 A QuickTime movie created in Adobe Premiere.

Windows creates a file extension called AVI, or Audio Video Interleave. This format, which was developed by Microsoft, provides similar functions to QuickTime on Windows compatible systems.

Apple has always maintained a close relationship with their software developers, thus ensuring that software products are compliant and will operate with the broad range of Macintosh CPUs that exist. This has been the case with QuickTime. QuickTime has proven to be a versatile format, allowing easy playback capabilities on almost all Macintosh models. Also, because QuickTime will also allow playback on Windows compatible systems, its popularity will flourish.

The fact that these formats exist and offer compatibility between platforms is an exciting side effect of the convergence of this technology. The distinction between which product will work on which platform is beginning to diminish, allowing the user to benefit from more simplified industry standards.

Creating QuickTime Movies

Acquiring video images and footage in your computer requires a large amount of hard disk space and sufficient amount of RAM. Also required is a video capture board and a software program that is capable of grabbing the video frames you want to save as a digital movie on your computer. After you have acquired the video files, you will need software that allows you to edit the movie. Such software includes Adobe Premiere.

Remember that when you are considering jumping into video production and editing, you must have ample hardware to make it work. Working with video requires adequate RAM and hard disk storage. This can be a part of your front-end purchase or can be easily added later. However, the initial addition is a good idea.

If your video source also contains sound, you will need a computer with a built-in sound input port. To capture video you must first make sure that your video and sound hardware are set up according to manufacturer's specifications (see Figures 9.9 and 9.10).

Figure 9.9 Once a digitizing board is added to the computer, audio and video can be captured.

Figure 9.10 External devices can plug into the computer through simple connectors.

Keep in mind that the quality of video and sound input will vary depending on the manufacturer of the board that you use. Also be aware that the quality of your source materials is very important. If you are importing video stored on a laserdisc with a high-quality video digitizing board, then the results of your imported video should be sharp and crisp and display excellent resolution. On the other hand, if you are using a second generation videotape as your source with a high-quality video input board, your final input resolution will not be enhanced further by having a higher quality board. Remember the old saying, "Garbage in, garbage out."

Equipment Requirements

Acquiring the proper components to capture the various media types and to implement them into a usable format may require a rather substantial purchase for the occasional video user. On the other hand, a serious user making his living in this arena will need to invest in the proper quality equipment for the job.

Figure 9.11 Some of the hardware peripherals that allow you to capture images to assemble digital audio and video.

Live video can be brought into the computer through a number of digitizing cards, manufactured by a variety of vendors. Computers with built-in A/V componentry have the ability to input and output video. Your level of involvement will play a key role in equipment decisions.

QuickTime presentations also have the capability to be copied onto videotape if your hardware supports the output of video. Keep in mind that the quality of your QuickTime video will probably be lower than your traditional video footage. At some point you will have to make the call on what is adequate video. QuickTime is capable of handling full screen images at 30 frames per second (fps) which is broadcast quality. Your hardware will definitely play a prime role here.

In order to make broadcast quality video, you will need a computer with a fast processor, a large hard drive, and good utilization of compression techniques and perhaps compression boards. To be a serious producer of QuickTime movies you should consider the biggest, best, and fastest hardware on the market. This will make your job as a producer easier.

Figure 9.12 Developing and capturing broadcast-quality video requires the right equipment.

Based on what your requirement for video footage might be, you have a couple of options. You can shoot your own video with either an industrial or consumer quality video camera, or you can have a professional videographer do the work for you. The general use of QuickTime has proven that a high-quality consumer video camera works well for a variety of requirements. Keep in mind your end product. Save the bucks you would have spent on a more expensive camera and invest it in more RAM. On the other hand, if you are going to produce corporate video and interactive presentations, then this issue may require reevaluation.

Another option for video acquisition is to purchase clip media. Like clip-art services and digital photo images that are available for your publishing programs, there are clip-media resources available for multimedia producers. These images often are arranged by categories and can offer much value and time savings if the product is applicable.

A/V or MPC Compatible Computers

Personal computers have changed with the times. In the past, a display, keyboard, and letter quality printer were sufficient for most jobs. Things are different today.

The personal computer is capable of producing anything from a pie chart to broadcast quality video.

Current products provide many options, especially in the realm of multimedia. With the variety of elements involved in multimedia production, the computer must be capable of bringing these elements in as well as sending them back out in one form or another.

As you know, there are dozens of companies that manufacture computers today. If you are relatively new to computing, the choices can be absolutely puzzling. One trend in computer choices today is the emergence of systems that contain more than just the CPU, monitor, and keyboard. Computer manufacturers are addressing the need for systems to include not only larger hard drives and faster processors, but also sound quality, video connectivity, and ability to interface with a variety of external devices.

One of the drawbacks of buying a system piece by piece is that you have an abundance of equipment to deal with. You may even find yourself at the office furniture store buying additional furniture items to support your ongoing computer peripheral purchases. On the other hand, buying piece by piece may be a good idea due to the need to connect each piece to another computer system. These independent components could also be compatible with laptop computers, providing expansion capabilities to these portable systems.

The hardware associated with the production of digital video and the rest of the total multimedia development process includes, but is not limited to the following:

- Computer

- Monitor

- CD-ROM drive

- CD-R (CD-ROM recorder)

- VCR (V-HS, S-VHS, 8mm, Hi 8)

- Speakers

- Tape backup system

- External AV drive

- Disk array

- Television monitor

- Video or Audio capture card

- Graphic or three-dimensional accelerator cards

As you can see, there are many devices that are a part of the desktop video process. What you need will vary based on to what extent you wish to go in your production.

If you are looking for simplicity in a computer system and would like to combine as many products and features as possible, an A/V or MPC system is worth investigating. A computer referred to an A/V unit would incorporate several basic audio/visual features in addition to the existing base computer configuration. In 1993, Apple Computer introduced their first A/V line, which consisted of the Quadra 840AV and the Centris/Quadra 660AV. As these machines were introduced, they immediately set new standards in integrated multimedia hardware technology and availability. These systems were a launching pad for several areas of technology in addition to audio and video features.

One good thing about the A/V computers is that they house many exciting technologies for the multimedia author or enthusiast. These systems also contain exciting features for the average business user, allowing them to have the functions of an office full of equipment contained in one computer system.

A/V computers also allow you to connect the computer to a television, camcorder, or VCR to record taped information or to capture live events. Though these early versions did a relatively poor job of exporting a clear video signal for television display, it still offered the capability. Other solutions such as third-party video card vendors, however, worked exceptionally well. This process works because of the compatibility between the Macintosh and traditional television sets. This capability alone is worth plenty if you are a casual or serious multimedia user or developer. After all, your productions may not always be viewed just on a computer screen. Occasionally you must present to a larger audience or output to videotape.

The inclusion of A/V technologies is not limited to Apple systems. Most major manufacturers, including IBM, Compaq, NEC, have chosen to integrate these technologies into some of their systems. These products have primarily been developed and marketed to enhance the value of their systems by offering components that are needed for a variety of purposes. These systems are primarily marketed to the small business and home arenas. A/V technology is good and certainly worth consideration. It is probably a good guess that this packaging of technologies will become more mainstream as time goes by.

These machines are a great value due to the amount of built-in features. You should, however, consider your budget and the quality of output before you purchase one of these units. If your primary need is for high-powered audio/visual output and input consider a powerful machine and an equally powerful video capture card. Your work environment may supply the extras mentioned as features in A/V machines and you would not need to clutter your system with many extras that you do not need.

MPC Standards

As previously mentioned, an MPC is a standard group of components on IBM and compatible systems designed for multimedia use. Many software programs indicate that they require your system meet certain MPC standards in order to operate properly, or perhaps to gain the maximum impact from the program. See Table 9.1 for MPC minimum standards.

MPC minimum standards may include:	
CPU:	25 mHz 486sx (or compatible)
RAM:	4 MB minimum (8 recommended)
Hard Disk Drive:	160 MB or above
CD-ROM Drive:	Double Speed (300k/sec sustained transfer rate)
	XZ ready/multi-session capable
	Enhanced drivers for better audio support
Audio:	16-bit audio card
	Music synthesizer
	On-board analog mixing
Video:	640 x 480 screen (minimum 13-inch screen)
	64k colors
I/O:	Serial and parallel ports
	MIDI in/out
	Joystick
Operating System:	Windows 3.0 (or higher)

Table 9.1

Video Digitizing Cards

With the advent of the technologies described above, numerous hardware products are being introduced to support and improve the process. Perhaps the most significant piece of hardware to do this is the video capture card. Video capture devices run from $200 to $20,000. For $200, you can buy a product like the "Snappy" frame grabber that allows you to capture still images into your system with up to 16.8 million colors on your PC. For $20,000, you can have a board that will do it all. For the average user inter-

Figure 9.13 A video digitizing board allows your computer to expand its capabilities to accept the importation of live or taped video information.

ested in obtaining quality video, the price tag is a bit more reasonable. For between $500 to $1,000, you can get a good board, capable of providing 16-bit color, with a frame rate of 30 frames per second.

The more expensive the board is, the more features you will get and better frame rate can be achieved. A 24-bit color and full-screen display, at 30 frames per second, is possible with boards in the $2,000 range. Something to consider in any video capture card is built-in compression. Compression takes the overall image file and reduces the information it has to process and then replaces it at the time it is being displayed. Having compression capabilities on the card means that the compression feature is a piece of hardware. This will provide better results than software-based compression. These better results are reflected through improvements in speed and image quality.

Another consideration for boards is Peripheral Component Interconnect (PCI) architecture compatibility. PCI is a high-performance expansion bus architecture developed by Intel. This hardware interface technology allows manufacturers to develop boards, such as video capture boards, that will work in either a Windows or Macintosh system (see Figure 9.13). A major benefit of the PCI bus is speed improvements in every area associated with throughput.

There are more than 200 vendors producing PCI cards, and over 500 cards are available that are compatible with the PCI bus architecture.

Like most computer products, video digitizing cards offer many variations in options and features. They also cover a wide spectrum of price ranges. They can be as low as $400 or as expensive as $5,000. As with most products, you get what you pay for. The $400 boards offer low-end capabilities, offering some of the same features of the more expensive boards, but lacking the quality components and interface that the better boards offer. The more expensive boards are capable of capturing full-motion video, rendering broadcast quality images.

It is probably not a good idea to purchase a video board based on what you read alone. If you have a chance, try it before you buy it, or at least have your local dealer or other professional advise you on your decision. Thoroughly examine your needs and what your final project will be. Know in advance what your end product is going to be, then take steps to get there.

Something to look for in a video card is its ability to handle future expansion. Many cards do not offer any type of expandability, outside of purchasing another card. On the other hand, some cards will allow you to expand them through a daughter-card addition. Often times, the warranty of the card will indicate if upgrades are available. Based on the model and company, you could be eligible for a free or reasonably priced upgrade Another area to consider is the life expectancy of the card. Is it current technology? Is it compatable with systems that run at 100mHz? at 200mHz? 300mHz? Make sure that it is compatible with a variety of system configurations. After all, you may be upgrading your system, and you want your card to grow with you.

Video Editing Software

Some features that video editing software might contain include:

- Special effects

- Dissolves

- Transitions

- Flying titles

- Animated logos

- Blue-screen

- Fade-in and fade-out

You are no doubt aware of the many competitors that offer solutions for word processing, drawing, spreadsheets, graphics, and other areas. When it comes to video editing software, there are also many companies that produce products for this task. As in other disciplines, there are companies that produce low-end as well as high-end solutions. Getting into this arena is based on what you plan to do, your budget, and your level of involvement.

From its introduction, the Macintosh has been a graphic-based computer. It is no surprise that it emerged early on as a logical choice to excel in the area of digital video. With the software development ties that Apple integrated early on in the development of QuickTime, the software and hardware products always worked in harmony. Due to this early lead, software companies also developed products for the Mac platform to support video editing processes. The PC on the other hand is growing at a phenomenal pace in the processes related to digital video. Today it is up to the user to decide his platform of choice and go from there.

Figure 9.14 Various media types can be integrated into video/audio editing software, allowing the creation of digital movies.

To become involved in basic video capture and editing, you can begin with very basic software. Typical video editing software will allow you to capture video directly into the program. Some computers come with bundled software that includes a very basic video capture application. This software will provide the ability to capture video but lacks additional options such as sophisticated editing features.

Video editing software will also allow the implementation of other media types in order to create a digital movie (see Figure 9.14). These media types can be virtually anything as long as they are able to be saved in an acceptable format. Scanned images, computer graphics, titles, background art, animation, sound, new video, and existing digital movies are all pieces that are able to be utilized to create new digital movies. Better editing software programs will accept these types of media. As this new field evolves, new and more sophisticated software will be offered.

Figure 9.15 Adobe Premiere is an easy to use tool for creating video on the Macintosh.

Capturing Video

To capture video, you must first have a source that provides video such as a VCR, camcorder, laserdisc, or still video camera.

You can record video images and sound directly to your computer using the proper hardware and software components. Software programs that support this process include Adobe Premiere. Premiere's software is specifically designed to create digital movies. It has sophisticated editing tools and supports the importation of video and sound through its movie and audio capture commands.

To record video from within Adobe Premiere, you need a video digitizing card with VDIG component software which is supplied by the manufacturer of the digitizer card, or an A/V or MPC system with this feature built in. If you want to record sound as well as images, you need a computer with a sound input port, or a sound digitizing device with input software such as the Audio Media board for

IBM and compatibles. Macintoshes with A/V capabilities allow sound-in and sound-out options.

Frame Rates

The rate option determines the maximum speed of the movie in frames per second (fps). The playback rate you actually achieve depends on the speed of your computer and hard disk and display card you are using. The higher the frame rate, the more lifelike the movement will appear. Image size is measured in pixels and frame rates in frames per second.

Compression

Compression is important to desktop video from the aspect of file size and replay on the screen. Motion J-PEG, or M-JPEG, is the most commonly used hardware compression format. MPEG-1 and MPEG-2 are also common compression methods. Fast and Wide SCSI-2 is currently the fastest mode of data transfer. Data transfer rates relate to compression because the faster the transfer rate from the storage device, the less the video file needs to be compressed.

NTSC

If you are going to be involved in multimedia, then you will need to know what NTSC is all about. NTSC is an acronym for National Television Systems Committee. This committee formulated the standards for United States color television systems. NTSC is the dominant broadcast standard in the United States and Japan, but is not used as commonly throughout the rest of the world. Phase Alternating Line (PAL) is the primary standard for most of Europe and Australia. Sequential Color and Memory (SECAM) is used in Eastern Europe, France, and the former Soviet Union.

When working with software and video cards, you will find that NTSC and PAL are typically supported. Many cards support SECAM as a standard and some offer it as an option. However most cards also accept other variations of NTSC video signals. For example, Composite mixes together the chrominance and luminance parts of the signal into one channel. S-Video is a two-channel video signal dealing with color and luminescence produced by high-end consumer and professional-level cameras such as S-VHS and Hi-8. RGB is a signal made up of three separate channels: red, green, and blue. There is a channel for each color plus a separate channel to synchronize each channel.

The A/V computers and video capture cards typically have NTSC output and input capabilities allowing the capture of video from domestic VCRs and camcorders as well as output to these units.

If you are working with software configuration that offer NTSC, PAL, and SECAM options, select the various options and observe the changes in the format as it appears on screen.

Capturing Still Images

Still images are transported into the computer in the same way that live video is. The only difference is that digital still cameras process static images. Static images are much smaller files than video images. A typical digital camera might store 32 standard-resolution images, or 16 high-resolution images in 24-bit color. They could also include both a Macintosh and Windows connecting kits. Digital still camera technology captures images to disk rather than to film. The images are stored on the disk until connected to the computer for image transfer.

Digital cameras start at approximately $400. They are innovative because the images can go directly to the computer for editing or for immediate use with no processing required. All you have to do is connect the camera to your computer and download the digital photo images. This type of product has been very effective in the area of real estate, insurance, and police investigation.

Digital Video Storage

Where and how to store your digital video files is an issue to be seriously investigated. In an environment where one second of digital video can consume more than the capacity of a single high-density floppy disk, other alternatives must be addressed to meet the storage demand.

When you work with digital video, you are working with many color pictures. These individual images can consume great amounts of disk space based on their size and image resolution. Producing a video clip that lasts only ten seconds may consume disk space in excess of five or ten megabytes.

As you research system configurations for desktop video, your computer should have a minimum 1 Gb hard disk drive on board. This will allow you to enter basic multimedia planning and design. The speed of the disk is also very important. The transfer rate should be several MB per second.

Storage Technology Types

SyQuest

Having auxiliary external storage devices is very important and often mandatory. Historically, one of the most popular external storage devices has been the SyQuest drive. SyQuest technology basically took the hard disk concept and made the disk removable, allowing subsequent disks to be used and removed at will. With the desktop publishing revolution of the 1980s, the need for additional storage grew rapidly due to the storage requirements of scanned images and the complexity of some documents. During this time, the SyQuest became a popular alternative because it was not a "fixed" storage solution. Because the media was modular, there were no limitations. Many service bureaus and trade shops have SyQuest drives, ensuring compatibility for just about everyone. This technology has grown in capacity. Earlier systems held 44 MB of data. The progression grew to 88, 105, 200, and then to 270 MB. This technology has served well through the years and is still a viable alternative.

Digital Tape

Digital tape is the most economical of the storage mediums. However, it is also the slowest. The advantage of digital tape is its high amount of storage capability. Examples of tape formats include 8mm and Digital Audio Tape (DAT). DAT is currently the most popular and interchangable, making it a good alternative.

ZIP Drive

If you are on a budget and are producing smaller multimedia projects, the Iomega ZIP drive is an excellent alternative. With a storage capacity of almost 100 MB per cartridge, it offers a great low-cost solution. The disks are magnetic and are about the size of a floppy disk. The unit costs under $20. and offers 100-MB cartridges. The 100-MB disks cost under $20 and are great for multimedia presentations. The drive is not the fastest for multimedia work, but it certainly has a variety of uses and you cannot beat the price.

JAZ Drive

The JAZ drive is related to the ZIP Drive. Basically, the Jaz Drive is the same product as the ZIP with the exception of the capacity. The Jaz Drive is available in both a 1 gigabyte and 2 gigabyte configuration.

Magneto Optical

Magneto Optical (MO) drives have been on the market for several years and continue to grow in popularity, primarily because they offer the lowest cost per megabyte of storage currently available, usually just a few cents per megabyte. Since their introduction, these devices have proven to be dependable storage devices. Many vendors promise their media has a shelf life of 100 years. Perhaps the drawback related to MO storage is that the access time is not as fast as other technologies. This aspect is improving continually to keep up with the demands that video requires for speed.

RAID

Redundant Array of Inexpensive Disks (RAID) are becoming very commonplace for professional digital video producers. RAID is interesting technology and has been pushed to sophistication because of the demands that video places on computer and storage systems. Video, as mentioned earlier, is intensive data, requiring that a lot of information be retrieved and processed for viewing virtually immediately. RAID systems work effectively because they store information in segments on the various drives and then the information is processed in a continuous manner. The result is a continuous flow of information to the computer screen.

An example of disk array configuration is as follows:

- Raid levels 0, 1, and 5

- Up to 30 MB per second transfer rate

- Plug-and-play convenience

- 8 Gb capacity

Technology Changes

Keeping up with technological changes in the computer field makes you continually search for what has been introduced or upgraded. Changes in screen displays, drive mechanisms, CD technology, peripherals, output devices, and the amazing amount of software will make your purchasing decisions even harder.

However, changes in technology are good for all of us. One good side effect is that usually the task we are learning today can be performed easier and faster tomorrow due to the constant improvements to technology.

The consumer video camera of the 1980s was a two-piece VCR that allowed the tape mechanism to be removed and taken into the field for use with a camera that was heavy and offered mediocre image quality. In contrast, the camcorder of today not only incorporates all of the features of this bulky equipment in a single lightweight unit, but some units offer near professional-quality video capabilities with worlds of special effects. With the advent of the digital camcorder, giant steps towards professional quality images are being achieved at a consumer level.

Today's computer technology continues at a fast rate of change. The Macintosh of 1984 was indeed revolutionary. It was compact and had a mouse, point-and-click simplicity, graphical interface, and many of the concepts that we are using today. However, current systems are many times faster and more colorful. They offer CD technology, can be used as fax machines, and incorporate voice recognition. They have excellent sound quality and you can output documents to various peripheral devices, making them revolutionary pieces of equipment. When you examine these changes, aren't you excited about the future of computing?

Chapter Ten

Animation

Making things move on your computer can be very simple, if you know which software makes it work. Establishing a reason for why something should move is important. Animation is a powerful medium if used at the proper time to communicate a point or message. Animation can be as simple as a two-dimensional logo entering and exiting from a presentation program, or as complex as a three-dimensional model with shading and rendering.

Animation carries unusual powers that allow the unreal, or even the unimaginable, to happen. The power of this medium is truly fantastic. The use of animation is also widely accepted by society as a whole. The fact that the Disney empire was built around animated characters is one testament to this. In the 1960s through the 1980s, the Disney studios significantly cut back on the number of animated features it produced because of the astronomical cost of producing a feature length animated movie. In the

1990s, Disney experienced a rebirth into the animation arena because of technological advances. What resulted was the emergence of several very popular animated films. This proves that the public has an interest in the powers of animation.

How does all of this impact what you will produce on your computer? In the realm of multimedia computing, animation is crucial. Remember that we are a part of the "TV Generation." We expect fast-paced movement, bright and colorful graphics, clear sound, and multiple images flashed before us in harmony. Lots of information in a short amount of time has become what we are accustomed to receiving.

Animation in Multimedia Computing

Animation from a major Hollywood movie studio is usually a major production. However, in its simplest form, animation is any movement on your computer screen. A title entering the screen from the right or left is a form of animation. A transition from one screen to another, utilizing a dissolve or curtain effect is a form of animation. Animation is simply movement. The following are three levels of animation used in multimedia presentations.

Level 1: Beginner

The beginner level requires no graphic experience. Perhaps the simplest and most commonly used form of computer-based animation comes in the form of presentation software. Programs such as Microsoft PowerPoint and Multimedia Design Corporation's mPower, provide an excellent platform for creating great looking presentations. These software applications also provide the capability to produce basic animated effects. These effects are crude in comparison to three-dimensional modeling software and programs like Macromedia Director, but nonetheless, any movement on the screen is still animation. Some of the effects you can expect from presentation software include:

Flying Titles

Titles and graphics enter from one location, pause, and then exit to another location.

Fade

Picture fade-in, fade-out, and movement.

Movement

Graphic objects can be set in motion by following a path that is invisible during the presentation mode.

Importation

Animated files can be imported into your presentation for playback at the user's discretion.

Another dynamic product that can effectively be used in the realm of animation is Apple's QuickTime. Quick-Time is very effective because once graphics are produced, they can be placed in frames in QuickTime format and played back as a movie, providing an animated sequence. As QuickTime plays a movie file, it is actually playing a series still images, at a predetermined frame rate, to achieve full motion. This works very effectively with computer illustrations and graphics as well. All of the timing and size controls are easily controlled by the user.

Level 2: Moderate

Moderate level requires an understanding of animation techniques and software. To create animation that is convincing and allows more sophistication than merely having a flying title move across a screen, you must be able

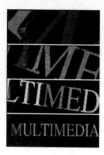

Figure 10.1 Using Apple's QuickTime for the playback of an animated sequence.

Figure 10.2 A series of images representing cell animation.

to have an understanding of cell animation techniques (see Figures 10.1 and 10.2). Cell animation refers to the various frames or individual pieces of artwork that make up an animated sequence.

Macromedia Director allows you to import a graphic and control where it is placed on the screen by using a timeline approach to animation. This form of sequencing a piece of art is very effective in creating animation with a single object. Objects can move from one screen location to another, and can also change size and shape along the way. Notice the space between the objects. This is normal in animation. When a series of graphic objects are played back at a proper speed, the movement appears to be smooth. The reason for this is even though the object has spatial gaps, when put in motion, the object appears to move fluidly. The reason for this is a phenomenon called perceived motion. This means that we anticipate that the character is moving, and therefore, we look beyond the small discrepancies between one position and the next.

This effect works differently based on the object. For example, if we see a cartoon of a character walking down the street, it is impractical to totally draw each minuscule movement to fully demonstrate the process. So, if the character is in a walking motion, then we are going to think that walking is what he is going to do, not fly or jump, but walk. Therefore, as the character proceeds, only certain steps are needed to ensure that the motion is that of walking.

The concept of perceived motion also applies to the utilization of digital movies. A digital movie is made up of individual cells containing snapshots from a video clip or other source of imagery. In the case of a QuickTime file consisting of digitized videotape, the play back via QuickTime is a series of images with gaps between each frame. Notice the differences between the sequential frames. The real trick is to play back these images at the required frame rate to ensure that the motion is perceived to be real.

If you are planning to import an animated file from one program to another, you will need to save the file in the proper format.

Level 3: Advanced

The advanced level of animation requires a full understanding and experience with modeling, graphic, and animation programs. This includes the ability to create two-dimensional and three-dimensional graphics, and understand how to put them in a sequence that allows them to perform as a believable character or event. There are numerous programs on the market today to support the creation of any character or scene imaginable. To become involved in this arena, you often need more cre-

Figure 10.3 This robot from the *Journeyman Project,* is imaged at intervals that create the illusion of fluid movement.

Figure 10.4 A screen from the *Journeyman Project,* demonstrating excellent three-dimensional animation techniques.

ativity than software proficiency. These programs are becoming easier to use and they support the idea process in an easy to use manner. Keep this in mind when considering the purchase of modeling software!

Multimedia titles like *The Journeyman Project* use realistic three-dimensional models and futuristic background images to transport the user into an entirely new environment (see Figure 10.4). We can go anywhere with the proper use of this technology and a little imagination.

Planning

Planning is an essential part of using animation in a multimedia production. As mentioned in Chapter 2, storyboarding is a requirement for any production. It is especially important when considering the insertion of an animated sequence.

File Formats

Animated files, like any other computer file, must be saved in various formats to be used in other applications. A single file can be saved as a PICT or .pct file. These images contain a smaller amount of information than normal. By utilizing several PICT or .pct files in an application such as QuickTime, an animated sequence or scene can be created. PICS files save graphic images in a series and allow playback in a sequence.

Morphing

Morphing is a phenomenon that continues to be popular in the presentation arena. Morphing has been used in Hollywood for many years to show the transformation from one image to another. This was one of the early special effects used in the movie industry. In reference to computer-based multimedia production, morphing has been around since the late 1980s and early 1990s. The morphing process allows the user to combine two images through an animated sequence that subtly changes the in-between images to simulate a gradual change from one to the other.

If you are familiar with the morphing process, you may not have thought of it as a form of animation. What makes it fit this category is the fact that there are numerous images that create the "in-between" sequence, which when played back at the proper speed, simulate real motion and a dynamic effect of reality. This form of animation is quite effective in showing a before and after scenario. Rather than merely showing the before image and

Figure 10.5 The morphing process must have a different start and end image.

then the after image, the first image gradually turns into the second (see Figure 10.5 and 10.6). This creates a dynamic effect.

The number of in-between images are specified by the user. The more in-between images that are specified, the better the transition appears. The boy to girl morph, shown in Figure 10.6, contains a total of 24 in-between images. The sequence shown here indicates in-between frames, numbers 6, 12, and 18.

Like all special effects, morphing should be used wisely and at the appropriate time. Using an effect like morphing over and over in a presentation could be serious overkill. Excessive use of morphing reduces its impact. Morphing, like other special effects, has its place. Use good taste and judgment when integrating into a presentation.

Animating the Computer Screen

Sometimes in the course of communicating your ideas, you will want to share a procedure that you have created on your computer. By far, the easiest way to do this is by using a product called CameraMan by MotionWorks software (see Figure 10.7). CameraMan is a screen recording utility that captures exactly what is happening on your screen to

Figure 10.6 As the morphing software generates the sequence, numerous "in-between" images are created.

a QuickTime movie. By assigning a key to start, stop, and pause, you can capture an on-screen process. CameraMan also has the ability to record voice narration and mouse clicks along with the screen movements in real time.

These QuickTime movies can be saved in various size formats, depending on how much memory is available. This process is invaluable for anyone interested in providing computer-based training.

Figure 10.7 CameraMan records your screen movements to a QuickTime file.

Part III

Producing/
Authoring/
Presenting

Chapter Eleven

Authoring Software

If you have ever had the responsibility to author any type of article or publication, then you are well aware of the challenges associated with putting together a group of words, sentences, and paragraphs that form a cohesive thought. As you contemplate the quest to become multimedia-literate, be prepared to broaden your present skill set.

As discussed in previous chapters, multimedia development involves the incorporation of many forms of media types. These media types only become a harmonious production when properly orchestrated. The way these files become properly orchestrated is through authoring software. As the word authoring suggests, you are the one telling the story.

Authoring software is a product that allows the development of a multimedia production by coordinating the various media types into a production. Instead of writing text for a book or publication, you are writing, composing, and assembling files for presentation on computers, televisions, VCRs, or perhaps a presentation to an audience. If you are a novice, then the thought of working in this type of environment may be intimidating. You may be an excellent illustrator or page layout designer but when it comes to making many elements work in harmony in the dynamic world of multimedia, you will find a series of new challenges.

How Does It Work?

If you are new at multimedia, and are confused about the buzzwords do not worry. Authoring software is very straightforward. Basically, authoring software allows you to take previously prepared graphics, sounds, animation, and movies, and place them under the control of one software program. Once they are connected by the authoring environment, the software allows you to take control, commanding the elements. In order for this to happen, the software must accept and execute your instructions.

Your external files do not necessarily become a part of the authoring software, but rather are controlled by the authoring software. For example, digital movies are traditionally very large files. When a movie is placed into the authoring program, it is usually linked to the original file, not recreated. Therefore, when you are copying a presentation or media production for distribution, the file created in the authoring software as well as the movie file must be together. When it comes time for the movie to be played, the software will look for the file for playback. Some programs, however, allow the option to place the entire movie file into the program.

Authoring software offers tremendous flexibility in the scope of what it can accomplish. Numerous products can be developed with authoring software. Some of these include multimedia presentations, CD-ROM titles, kiosks, computer-based training, artistic visualizations, and web pages.

Authoring programs are somewhat hybrid products: a cross between presentation programs and a programming language. The programming process varies in complexity based on the aptitude of the user and the type of end product that will be developed. The programming aspects related to multimedia authoring software usually refer to simple commands, or visual elements that allow you to tell your previously prepared files what to do, and when to do it.

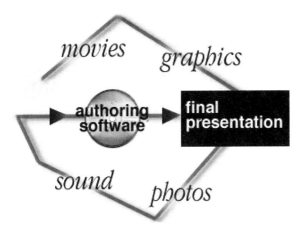

Figure 11.1 Previously prepared files are placed into authoring software to develop a media production.

As you will discover in your research, authoring programs usually offer either scripting options in a timeline format, or icon-based interfaces. When you look at a program that relies on scripting, you get the feeling that you are involved in programming. This is because the program relies exclusively on your input to tell objects what to do and when to do it.

Authoring Software Categories

In this section, we are going to examine a variety of software applications that allow development of interactive presentations and products. These applications include both presentation and traditional authoring software. A conscious decision has been made to add presentation software to this section. Traditionally, these products are grouped separately.

Presentation software has grown to the point of including some rather sophisticated features, including interactivity, branching, and acceptance of a variety of media types. These advances have elevated the capabilities of these programs making them much more than mere slide show applications.

Minimum Production Requirements

You can enter the authoring process in its most basic form by developing a project in a presentation program. Even though you may not create a high level of interactivity and may not use a variety of media types, presentation programs have a place in the multimedia process and support the authoring mind-set.

If you have been involved in computing for a while, then you remember when word processing programs were used only to produce typed pages. Today, word processing programs have grown in sophistication to incorporate graphic design tools, page layout capabilities, charting, and even the importation of multimedia elements such as digital movies. Now that presentation programs have been around for a while, they too are growing in capabilities. These programs now incorporate linking, animation, interactivity, Web page design, and much more. In fact, some of these programs rival what used to be considered sophisticated authoring environments.

Some presentation programs have the ability to launch other applications from within a presentation. Traditional slide-show software and interactive applications have merged somewhat over time, providing greatly enhanced features. The extendibility of these programs is growing, in some cases rivaling full-blown authoring programs, and increasing in sophistication with each new release.

Another great feature of these programs is their ease of use. If you need to get up and running in a short period of time, the typical presentation program will allow you to

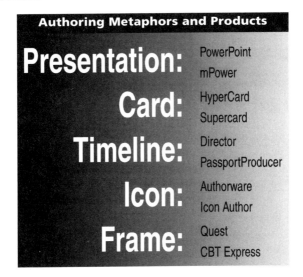

Figure 11.2 Different presentation and authoring environments listed by product class.

quickly develop an above average presentation. These programs usually contain a wide assortment of pre-designed background art as well as a variety of clip-art files that will assist in the assembly of a presentation. This is a great feature, especially if you do not have the time or resources to develop these elements yourself.

Another tremendous advantage is the ability to make your presentation compatible with other systems. Through the utilization of player technology, presentations can be saved, and made playable on both Macintosh and Windows systems. A player is basically the part of the software that allows playback only. Players do not include the ability to create presentations. This feature has been around for a while on high-end authoring software and is becoming a standard process for presentation software as well.

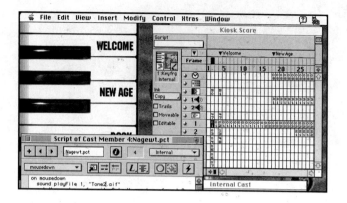

Figure 11.3 This screen represents scripting in Macromedia Director. Director is an example of an authoring software environment that uses a timeline format.

Better Production Requirements

Timeline-based authoring solutions, as shown in Figure 11.3, allow for extremely flexible functioning in an authoring software. Many of these programs offer features that allow the creation and control of many external devices, such as laserdisc, VCR, and audio equipment.

Typically, these environments offer the ability to be controlled through means of a script. These scripts tell the variety of external elements exactly what to do and when to do it (see Figure 11.4).

Such programs should have the ability to create, integrate, and synchronize the wide assortment of production elements. These elements include text, still graphics, animated graphics, video, and sound files. This class of software should also support the development of dynamic presentations, which include interactive marketing productions, entertainment media, demo disks, educational CD-ROM titles, information kiosks, technical visualizations, and the ability to print, or output, to videotape. This level of authoring has the capability to develop pages for the World

Figure 11.4 An example of a script using the Lingo scripting language in Macromedia Director.

Wide Web. The advantage of this technology is that the Web page can contain sound, animation, and interactivity, allowing the user to benefit from multimedia technology. The ability to link and control external devices, such as VCRs, laserdisc, and audio compact-disk players is also a feature that should be in this class of authoring software.

Ultimate Production Requirements

Ultimate authoring software includes all the features listed thus far and more. Additional features include the ability to create computer-based training programs. These programs would allow the user to save a training session at any point and would contain the capability to capture or to track user responses and progress.

Enhanced capabilities in kiosk settings are also a feature of high-end authoring environments. Through advanced capabilities, kiosk interfaces can collect information about demographics, personality profiles, age, and other information and store it in a database.

Cross-platform development and connectivity to a vast array of external devices is also integral to high-end solutions.

Product	mPower
Company	Multimedia Design Co.
Platform	Macintosh/Power Macintosh/Windows 95
Class	Presentation/Authoring/Interactivity
Special Features	Produces player files
	Can digitize audio and video
	Controls externals: CD-Audio and VCRs

Table 11.1 Presentation Software

A Closer Look

Before we go in depth, let us take a look at some specific products, their general classification, and compatibility. The product selection represents a broad category of products that offer similar features and functioning. The selected products give a good overview of features that comparable products offer.

Presentation Software • mPower

mPower is one of those rare products that newcomers to presentation and multimedia development will be happy to discover. This unique application creates an environment that removes the intimidation from the development process. Multimedia Design Corporation took the point-and-click metaphor that is predominant with the graphical user interface (GUI) and applied it to this presentation/authoring solution. mPower is presently a Macintosh-only product. By using the mPower Player application, presentations can be saved in a format that will play on Macintosh and Windows systems.

Figure 11.5 The mPower menu is made up of simple buttons that link to other options.

Creating a new presentation, adding a background, sound or graphic, and creating a player file are all done by merely clicking a button. This program offers much power and is perhaps underrated when it comes to its visibility in the marketplace. mPower has the sophistication to capture audio and video components from within the application. Also included is the ability to control externals, such as CD players, laserdisk players, and VCRs. The ability to launch other applications from within mPower also exists. This is done by attaching a hot button which will open the application or document of your choice.

Some features that are found in mPower include:

- Digitize sound and video from VCRs, laserdisc, and video cameras (providing the computer is equipped with a digitizing card)

- Control of various external media devices, such as CD players, VCRs, and laserdisc players

- Create digital movies

- Play video clips from external VCRs

- Integrate audio from CDs, microphones, or external sound files

- Import or launch PowerPoint or Persuasion files

- Import PICT, PICS, PCX, Kodak PhotoCD, and EPS files

- Integrate charting

- Branching capability through hot buttons

- Video chalk for highlighting during presentation

- Royalty-free Player distribution

Authoring Software • Director

The first product on the market was Macromedia Director. The company was previously called MacroMind and the product was called VideoWorks. Around 1985, this product burst onto the market, offering an array of features for creating and controlling animation that was very unique. At that time, we were not accustomed to having much more on our computer screens than word processing, database, spreadsheet, or simple graphic software applications. Since that time, Macromedia has grown into the leading software company producing multimedia and related software products. VideoWorks has evolved into Director and is available for both Macintosh and Windows compatible computer systems.

Director is one of the most powerful authoring, design, and animation products available. Some of the fea-

Product	Director
Company	Macromedia
Platform	Macintosh/Power Macintosh/ Windows/Windows 95
Class	Authoring/Interactivity/ Computer-Based Training
Special Features	Excellent animation control, timeline interface

Product	Authorware
Company	Macromedia
Platform	Macintosh/Power Macintosh/ Windows/Windows 95
Class	Authoring/Interactivity/Computer-Based Training/Course Development
Special Features	Icon-driven interface, control of external devices, Computer-Based Training design

Table 11.2 Authoring Software

tures include a painting program, transitions, special effects, and digital video importation and control. There are also two sound channels for either music or narration. Director contains an object-oriented scripting language called Lingo. This language allows for custom control without requiring the extensive knowledge of a programming language.

Director can be used for Corporate presentations, CD-ROM titles, kiosk, visualizations, training disk, and even simple slide shows.

Figure 11.6 Director offers a scripting language called Lingo, which controls the variety of multimedia elements.

Macromedia has developed the concept of "author once and playback anywhere." This concept goes beyond Macintosh and Windows compatible to other areas that include the Internet, corporate intranets, set-top players, and other operating systems. Director is 100 percent binary compatible format, allowing productions developed on one computer to be played on another platform.

Authoring Software • Authorware

Macromedia Authorware Professional maintains a leadership standard much like its sibling Director. Authorware Professional offers an iconic interface that controls complex applications and interfaces without the need for scripting. The icons are placed along a flowline so that

Figure 11.7 The icon-based interface for Authorware Professional.

events happen in a logical sequence (see Figure 11.7). This controls various events like audio, video, interaction, and transitions. You click and drag icons as opposed to using a programming language such as Lingo in Director.

When you choose to run a program, you are prompted to link the appropriate file that you desire to play or display and the files are properly linked. Authorware also has the ability to play interactive movies that were created in Director. This type of compatibility is one advantage of the same company developing related products. Authorware excels at CBT applications due to the fact that it allows a high level of sophistication in the area of interactive branching and managing user feedback information (see Figure 11.8).

Authorware also contains the ability to control externals such as laserdisc players, CD audio players, and VCRs.

Authoring Software Functioning

Authoring software, by its very nature, must be able to not only accept outside files and put them into some form of action or organization, but it must also be extendible, performing functions beyond its typical self-contained features. Many of these programs will contain the capability to go beyond the limits of accepting what you have placed in them, and controlling what they do, and when they do it. The more serious applications will contain the ability to access and control video from a VCR or a laserdisc, open an external application, or be used as a reliable solution for a touch-screen kiosk environment.

The more sophisticated authoring programs typically incorporate additional functioning above and beyond the ability to just control a presentation. Many have the capability to edit existing files or to create externals from within the program. mPower, for example, allows the user to capture video or sound from external sources, save the file, and use it within the program, or with other programs. Director has a built-in painting program and Persuasion has the capability to create Web presentations. All of these products contain the ability to extend beyond their core functioning.

These features will vary from program to program. Often the more sophisticated the features and add-ons are, the more the program will cost. Keep this in mind when considering what authoring environment is best for your application. Typically, built-in programs, such as the painting program in Director, are not powerful, full-featured applications, but are extremely useful when the need arises to perform a quick graphic touch-up in a presentation.

Figure 11.8 In authoring software, previously prepared components can be orchestrated to present and playback on demand.

Enhanced Functioning Example

Figures 11.9 through 11.12 explain how mPower allows the capture of video from within the application. This type of built-in feature gives the user a fairly comprehensive tool to do more than just assemble the traditional elements normally included in a presentation. When reviewing an authoring program, look for maximum functioning. Make sure the features will handle your immediate requirements as well as allow future growth.

Figure 11.9 A video source is selected from the "attached components" menu.

Figure 11.10 Peripherals and ports selected.

Figure 11.11 The movie image size is selected.

Figure 11.12 Options are available allowing you to choose what to do with the video.

Software products that contain the ability to link to external devices such as this are good examples of how the authoring environment can add additional functioning to its original purpose. Often, features such as the ability to capture video and audio are provided by external software applications. Having these capabilities built in to one program is a real benefit. Ensure, however, that the functioning of these added features is up to the quality level to support the quality of work you must accomplish. These additional features will assist in the decision making process of what authoring software will do the job for you.

File Formats

Even though authoring programs are capable of producing various types of files from within the program, traditionally, they are intended to accept files prepared previously in other applications. In order to incorporate these files into the authoring environment, they must be saved in a format that the authoring program can recognize.

Back in the old days, software developers introduced a product with basic save formats. In the mid 1980s, there were not as many options or as much need to integrate one file format into another as there are today. Valuable software products typically endured long enough to go through several version upgrades. These products usually have the need to be integrated with other products. The longer a product stays on the market, the more other products will grow around it, and will want to take advantage of the ability to import or export information.

This concept became quite evident during the desktop publishing revolution. Early versions of page layout programs would accept only limited file formats such as Bitmap, PICT, TIFF, and so on. In order for other application files to be placed directly into these layout programs, they had to offer the specific formats that the page layout program would accept. Figure 11.13 demonstrates this point.

This same concept holds true for multimedia authoring software. This concept, however, continues to grow in scope with the addition of new products and peripherals. In an authoring environment, numerous file types will be imported from a variety of software applications. Some examples are listed in Table 11.3. Table 11.4 provides a brief description of file formats, their function, and their abbreviated names.

PAGE LAYOUT APPLICATION

SCAN... bitmapped images saved in a compatible format for importation.

TEXT... created in a word processing application and saved as a text file

ART... created in an illustration program and saved in a compatible format.

Figure 11.13 Page layout programs can accept externally prepared files saved in an acceptable file format.

FILE TYPE	FILE EXTENSION
Art/Graphic	.bmp, .pct, .eps, .cdr, .gif, .il5, PICT, PICT2, EPS, TIFF, GIF, RIFF
Animation	PICS
Sound	.AIF, .WAV
Movie	.mov, .avi
Portable Document	.pdf
Compression	.jpg, .mpg
Web Page	.html

Table 11.3 File types that can be imported into authoring software environments.

EXTENSION	FUNCTION
.pct or PICT	Line or bitmapped art files
PICT2	Line or bitmapped art files—a wider variety
.eps	PostScript line art files from Adobe Illustrator or Macromedia Freehand, or bitmapped art files from Adobe Photoshop
.tif or TIFF	Files saved in this format can be placed into a page layout program
.gif	The standard graphic file format for on-line services
pics	A series of graphics, often in sequence, that can be imported for playback in an animated sequence
.aif	An audio file format
MIDI	Musical Instrument Digital Interface—allows instrument sounds to be captured digitally directly into the computer
.jpg	Joint Photographers Experts Group—A format for compressing the size of graphics files
.mpg or MPEG	Motion Picture Experts Group—A standard for the compression and playback of digital movies
MPEG 2	Motion Picture Experts Group—An advanced standard for the compression and playback of digital movies capable of making the images appear more lifelike, with greater resolution and image clarity
.mov	QuickTime files for Macintosh and Windows
.pcx	PC bitmap file format–Old format, no compression
.bmp	PC bitmap file format—Introduced with the advent of Windows. They are not compressed —easily opened with Windows Paint and PC Paintbrush. BMP will easily integrate with Mac programs.
.avi	Audio/Video Interleave—Allows video to be played back by QuickTime for Windows.
.bin	Uncompressed Movie
.mci	Media Control Interleaves–Allows IBM and compatibles to control vcrs, laserdisc, cd players, etc.

Table 11.4 *(opposite)* Various file extensions and their functions.

Authoring on One System for Distribution on Another

As mentioned earlier in the book, a convergence of technologies is taking place. Just a few years ago, the very thought that you could develop a multimedia presentation on a Macintosh and be able to play it on an IBM or compatible machine was absurd. However, thanks to hardware and software advances and vendor agreements and co-development endeavors, this capability has become a reality.

Player technology is changing the method of delivery for the presentations we are churning out these days. Often times these player files are referred to as "players" or "projectors." A player file allows the presentation to be "packaged" with enough of your program development code to be played back on other machines. Machines that the player file is distributed to are not required to own the software in which your presentation was developed. Projector is the metaphor that Macromedia uses for Director files. These projectors typically have an icon that looks like a projector. Since the Macintosh and Windows operating systems are icon-driven interfaces, the projector typically indicates that this is a self-running presentation.

Since we have come this far in technology and in partnerships, you can look forward to even easier delivery of your products on multiple platforms in the future. The next step in this evolution is for software developers to produce authoring programs that will allow you to develop a production once that can be read by either Macintosh or IBM compatibles without developing a "player" file format.

Another consideration with player files is that some companies require that you pay a royalty for files that you prepare and distribute via their player technology. This is a serious consideration if you plan to develop and distribute

Figure 11.14 The ability to develop on one platform and play back on another allows wide distribution.

to a mass audience. Some software developers initially used this strategy, then opted to drop it in order to reach a wider, more profitable market with their software products instead of player licensing fees. Look for this trend to continue.

Multimedia Cross Platform

If you have been computing for a while, you will know that the term does not have the fear attached to it that it once did. With file sharing and information becoming more widespread in recent years, software and hardware developers have navigated through the once difficult task of communicating from one operating system to another.

At one time, the traditional idea of working cross-platform meant that you could transfer a data file from one system to another. Other cross-platform issues related to situations such as saving a Macintosh page as a PostScript file in order to have it opened in a PC-compatible program.

Back in the early 1990s, developing media applications for the Macintosh required Mac-specific components. The same held true for IBM and compatibles. This is not true today. More and more software applications are supporting the ability to develop a multimedia production on one system and distribute on multiple systems.

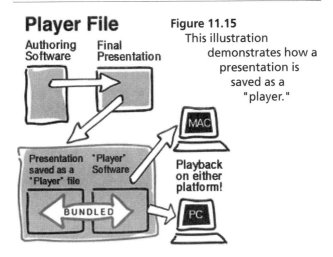

Figure 11.15
This illustration demonstrates how a presentation is saved as a "player."

Multimedia developers are looking to use their current set of development tools to produce titles and products that have the ability to be marketed to the masses with multiple platform compatibility. The Player technology is certainly one concept that is making this happen.

Multimedia Production End Results

When you author a project, you will have a specific goal or purpose. If you are anxious to learn what direction you can take with a specific product, here are some ideas.

- Games
- Interactive laserdisc
- CD-ROM creation
- Web site/page development
- Game cartridge development
- Multimedia network
- Simulations/prototypes
- Computer-based training

The Best Development Platform

What is the best automobile? What is the best airline? What is the best hotel chain? What is best is up to the person using a given system or software. If you began computing or developing media on a Macintosh, then chances are that is your platform of choice. If this is true, then you may have difficulty working with Windows because you are not accustomed to the environment or may not have the opportunity to be comfortable with it. This also works in reverse.

What is happening with the convergence of hardware and software technologies is that the look and feel of software applications on either the Macintosh or IBM and compatibles is becoming somewhat identical. This allows the user, no matter what platform is being used, to work in virtually the same environment.

The Macintosh was the platform of choice for development early on due to the fact that most of the graphic and multimedia products were initially developed to take advantage of its graphic and sound capabilities. With the introduction of Windows, software and hardware developers were anxious to create products for these systems. This was a particular advantage for software developers due to the fact that there were far greater numbers of IBM and compatibles in the marketplace. The result of the available products for both platforms has assisted in the explosion of multimedia as a whole.

Chapter Twelve

Interactivity

Interactivity means that the user takes control of the media and the options presented to him or her. By doing this, the user can seek specific information he desires to study, research, or review. This method of direct access allows the user to attain specific information without going through other data that may not be relevant to his information quest.

Interactivity means that the program responds to you. It asks you a question and waits until you answer. In multimedia, when you press a button, something will happen, such as:

- A background or slide will change

- An audio or video clip will play

- A transition will happen

- You can enter or exit the presentation

This chapter will review how interactivity is important to the multimedia design process.

Interactivity, in terms of computer-based multimedia, refers to an action that the user makes to control the events being viewed on the screen.

Determining the
Need for Interactivity

Why is interactivity important to the multimedia process? The utilization of video has been around for many years now. Video is a part of our daily lives. We rent movies to watch on our VCRs, we create movies with our camcorders, we use videotape training movies at work, and we use videotape to create product advertising and promotion. You could say that video is a highly used form of media woven into the fabric of our daily lives.

Video is good, video is effective, video is everywhere, but there is one thing that traditional video is not. Video is not interactive!

Despite the many positive aspects of video, it is not an interactive medium. Most of us have had the opportunity to view a training video. Many of these videos are well done, providing pertinent information to the task at hand. But for some, the full content of the video can be totally absorbed, while for others, only a certain percent can be retained. The reason for this is that we all learn at different levels and in different ways.

A remedy for this could be to have the user rewind the tape and view it over. Or instead of reviewing the entire tape, the viewer could view just details that were missed on the first run through. This could be a problem, however, if you are a part of a group viewing the tape. There may not be the opportunity to view it again or you may not be able to find the right spot on the tape.

What is the alternative to videotape and how does interactivity come into the picture? CD-ROM-based multimedia is an excellent method for creating or distributing information that users can interact with and move at their own pace. These CD-ROMs can be in the form of a disk that is compatible with a computer, a set-top player, or even a game machine.

Our society has reached a level where users are used to instant gratification as far as quenching their desire for obtaining information when they want it. Interactivity with computer-based information is becoming the norm. To support this, look at the popularity of the Internet!

Some media visionaries are predicting that in the near future, we will be able to interact with movies, changing the story line and affecting the outcome of the plot. Many of us have been involved with interactivity since we were kids by choosing the many options found in a home video game system. We also interact with our televisions in the form of choosing what channel we will watch and if we want to record the program on our VCRs.

In the realm of multimedia, interactivity is not only critical, it is mandatory to the process. Multimedia depends on developing a user interface that has a pleasing look and intuitive feel, enticing the user to become involved. Once the user gets there, however, he needs to know where to begin and how to carry on.

The very nature of interactive multimedia means that you will constantly see a different look and feel with each product. It is important from a development standpoint, that the user interface be based upon a common sense approach, allowing the user to automatically know how to use the product at first glance.

Action/Reaction

Usually, the user takes the initiative to begin the interaction process with the computer screen. This action could be prompted by a sound, graphic, or video that may be coming from the unit.

What happens after the user responds to an on-screen prompt by clicking or touching a button or graphic? This is based on what the button or graphic is programmed to do. Some software programs offer a limited number of options

Figure 12.1 The domino effect of what happens once an interactive button is selected.

that the user can choose to make an object respond to interactivity. In more sophisticated authoring programs, what you can produce is limited only by your creativity. Figure 12.1 illustrates the sequence of events to make an action respond interactively. In this scenario, the user finds a digital movie file and makes it come to the screen and play.

Another example of what happens after the button is selected is shown in Figure 12.2. When the interactive button is selected, various events happen to retrieve the file, display it, initiate a transition, and then move on to another similar sequence. These interactive buttons can be any graphic element, or area, on the screen.

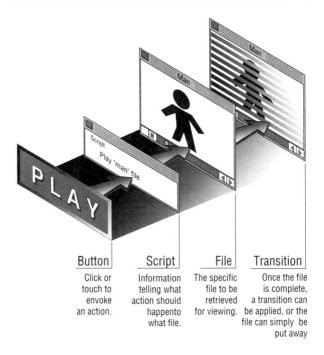

Button	Script	File	Transition
Click or touch to envoke an action.	Information telling what action should happento what file.	The specific file to be retrieved for viewing.	Once the file is complete, a transition can be applied, or the file can simply be put away

Figure 12.2 What lies behind an interactive button.

Creating a button that will provide a programmed response can be simple or complex, based on what you want the response to be. The complexity is determined by the software application being used. For example, some applications use the hot button approach. The mPower software is an example of an application that uses the hot button concept. This process allows the user to cover a certain portion of a graphic with an invisible hot button. When this area is selected in playback mode, it will invoke

Figure 12.3 mPower offers easy to use hot buttons to execute commands. When viewed normally, these buttons are invisible.

an action that is preprogrammed by the author (see Figure 12.3).

Director works in a similar manner, and offers vast extendability. An excellent example of how a real interactive button works is in Exercise 1 on the CD-ROM. Figure 12.4 demonstrates that a graphic of a piano key will be used as an interactive button. A script will be written to make this key perform a specific function.

Figure 12.4 In Director, any object can become a button.

Figure 12.5 The Script, from Directors Lingo scripting language, gives instructions as to what will happen next.

The script, in the case of Director, is what makes the interactive process begin. Any time any portion of the graphic is selected, the script immediately goes into effect. The processes described in the script can vary greatly. Functions like pauses, advances, play sounds, and others can be added to create a custom interactive function (see Figure 12.5).

When developing a multimedia production, using the proper software for the job is crucial.

How Complex Is Your Need?

If you choose software to produce a project, first determine what the project will involve. If your task is to develop a slide presentation, both presentation software and full-featured development software will accomplish this. Naturally, there are cost differences between the two. Perhaps the determining factor as to what to use will lie in what your long-term usage will be. You may find that the purchase of both will be required.

Chapter Thirteen

Presentations To Go

The day of doing business in our local community only is long gone. We have been in the jet age for quite some time now, and doing business around the world is commonplace. Because of this, marketers, educators, instructors, and the rest of us must be able to tell our stories, present our wares, and entertain an audience in a variety of venues.

Taking a presentation on the road is nothing new. What is new and exciting is the proliferation of products entering the marketplace that make these presentations look better, sound better, and easier to use. Traditional slide presentations are great, but the only last minute modifications that can be done to them is the reorganization of the slides themselves, not the information on the slide. One of the truly great benefits of having presentation material in a computer file is that the information can be modified by the end user right up to the last minute.

Mobile Multimedia

Because so much business is done in remote locations, notebook computing has become a highly effective method of delivering quality presentations. In many cases, the actual presentation is not developed on the notebook but rather on a desktop computer. Once the project is developed and perfected, it is copied onto the notebook and then the road show begins.

Often times, we find that notebook models have limitations. They may not be as fast, able to display in higher resolutions, have better color, or integrate video as desktop units can. Earlier notebook models left a lot to be desired as far as their capability to be used as comprehensive presentation systems. They would handle simple slide-to-slide presentations, but were not capable of more sophisticated, fully integrated multimedia action. For the average professional who does not want to learn how to integrate these elements, the quest for the all-in-one solution with plug-and-play simplicity is never ending.

The great thing about notebook computers today is that they are real computers, comparable in speed and features to many desktop models. Perhaps the only limitation is their screen display. These displays are good, and getting better all the time, but they cannot compare to an RGB monitor. Obviously, they are not designed to compete with a desk-bound monitor, but rather provide a display designed for casual or occasional use. A good feature of most notebooks is that they can connect to your desk-bound unit allowing you to view a presentation or use the full functioning of your notebook at your desktop.

Due to their sophistication, notebook computers are in great demand. As a result of this high demand, more energy has been placed in the development of better units with even more sophisticated componentry. Screen displays are getting brighter and bigger, hard disk capacity rivals desktops, and processor speeds are equally as fast as desktop counterparts. With these capabilities it only makes sense that other desktop components become an integral part of notebooks. Current notebooks contain CD-ROM drives, sound cards, speakers, and all of the necessary connectivity to external devices. With these powerful enhancements and connectivity options, notebooks are logical products for controlling mobile presentations (see Figure 13.1).

If travel is a part of your future plans, you may want to consider the following for your mobile computing needs. As mentioned before, the new generation of notebook computers are extremely powerful, containing desk-bound com-

Figure 13.1 Notebook necessities for mobile multimedia.

puter capabilities. If you plan to take a multimedia presentation on the road, you must be assured that your system is capable of delivering the content you are presenting. As you know from your research, your desk-bound computer must have lots of hard disk space, a lot of RAM, and a fast processor. These requirements will vary based on your view of a typical multimedia presentation. That is, if you need to show a simple slide show, then your requirements will be modest. If you need to create an extensive presentation with interactivity, scripting, heavy graphic usage, and digital video integration, then you need to add all the bells and whistles.

Here are three words of advice for anyone taking a presentation on the road: research, research, research! Research your products, their advantages, uses, and their connectivity options and limitations. Research thoroughly your presentation location and learn as much as possible about the physical environment of the presentation space. Research the hardware, software, connections, and peripheral devices that you will use. Experience can be the best teacher, but proper research and rehearsal will benefit you greatly.

If presentation design is going to be performed on a desktop computer with the actual presentation given from a notebook, make sure that an in-house run-through is performed on the notebook to ensure compatibility and speed consistency. If the desktop unit is a fast machine, time and energy can be spent on making sure that settings, transitions, and other features work well. However, if the notebook system has a slower processor, hard drive, and other system architecture differences, do not expect the presentation to work the same. Make sure that time is devoted to thorough testing on the system that will be used for the actual presentation. Multimedia development on a notebook may not be an ideal scenario, but being able to perfect your presentation is critical.

Following is a feature checklist and suggestions for notebook computers used for media presentations:

- 750MB hard drive minimum

- PCMCIA cards slots

- CD-ROM drive (either internal or external)

- Extra batteries

- 16MB RAM minimum

- Connectivity to external monitors

- Monitor mirroring capability

- Sound card capabilities

- Internal speakers and connections for external speakers

- Internal microphone

- Docking station connectivity

Figure 13.2
Expanding the capability of a notebook through connectivity to a docking station.

— Laptop

— Docking Station

The ability to add multimedia enhancements to a notebook computer increases a system's flexibility. The addition of a docking station, which provides extras like enhanced sound features, speakers, CD-ROM drives, and enhanced external connectivity, is a real benefit. For notebooks that do not have these features built in, this is an excellent option (see Figure 13.2).

- Motion Picture Experts Group (MPEG) compression technology is an important factor in helping the notebook become a viable factor in mobile presentations. MPEG should be hardware-based for optimum performance.

- If sound is an important part of your presentation, and you are using a PC-compatible system, SoundBlaster 16-bit compatibility is needed. This, in combination with external speakers, will produce the best audio results.

- If working from a CD-ROM drive, it should be the fastest possible. However, if your presentation can fit on a hard disk drive, you will yield better performance in speed.

- Products such as CD-ROM drives and internal hard drives should be easily upgradeable.

- Prices for multimedia equipped notebooks range from around $2,000 to $8,000.

Presentation Devices

Most equipment today is designed with portability in mind, to appeal to the user's decision to take it wherever he wants, even if there are no plans to use it in a remote setting. This technology is lighter, smaller, and better. Sales representatives are prime candidates for this technology due to their demand to present products and facts to a crowd.

Connectivity to peripheral devices is what makes presenting in a remote location work. At our office or place of work, we connect our systems into printers, network servers, speakers, and other devices. On the road, we may have the same needs. However, the needs are even more diversified. Beside having the need to connect to local devices to make the presentation happen, there are other hardware connectivity options that must be addressed. Figure 13.3 and the following demonstrate devices that are a part of mobile multimedia.

LCD Panels

LCD panels have been around for several years. They offer high-resolution display and good quality. LCD panels have become a staple in the presentation arena due to the fact that many companies own one and they are easy to obtain through audio/visual rental agencies. Also, most hotels or educational environments have an overhead projector on their premises, making it easy to deliver a presentation.

LCD Projectors

LCD projectors have changed recently and are setting new standards in brightness and clarity in a small, self-contained box. Early LCD projectors were very large and expensive, and only had mediocre display brightness and color density. Newer projectors weigh in the neighborhood of 10 pounds.

Figure 13.3 Some of the devices that connect to computers to make presentations happen.

Features of LCD projectors should include:

- 640 x 480 pixel resolution

- 16.7 million colors

- 18-inch to 300-inch screen size

- S-Video Input

- RCA audio and video input

- Built-in speaker

- Remote control

- Compatibility with Macintosh and IBM & Compatibles

- NTSC, PAL, S-VHS compatibility

RGB (3-Gun) Data Projectors

These projectors project the biggest and brightest image currently available, due to their size and complexity. They are sometimes referred to as a 3-gun unit because they have three glass lenses on the front that project independent red, green, and blue images to form a full-color image. These units are capable of projecting either from the front or rear, from a desktop, or ceiling. This solution provides the optimum in quality, but the maximum in handling and inflexibility. These units are typically rented by the day with the base rate including a technician. The technician is required due to the temperamental nature of the unit. If your presentation requires the best, this is the way to go.

Direct View Monitors

Direct view or presentation monitors range from 27 inches to 42 inches in screen size. These monitors offer excellent resolution and color depth, making them a logical choice for smaller audiences demanding the best possible output. Prices range from $2,500 all the way up to $14,000. These monitors support traditional NTSC signals for television and movie viewing, as well as computer data input. Better monitors support NTSC and computer interfaces simultaneously. Many monitors also offer built-in speakers, but having the option to connect external speakers is a benefit.

Controlling Your Presentation from a Distance

Slide projectors have offered remote control capabilities for many years. Presenters, storytellers, and salespeople have benefited from this feature, which allows the presenter to be at a location other than that of the projection device. Contemporary presentation technologies pro-

Figure 13.4 A wireless controller substitutes for a mouse.

vide products that also conform to the desire of the presenter, allowing him to give a presentation without being chained to the presentation device.

All presenters are different. Some prefer to remain at a podium because of a comfort level they feel standing behind something. Some may be required to stand by their computers due to the constraints of the presentation environment or because they are forced to stay with their machine in order to click the mouse to advance a slide in the presentation. Then there are others that want to have the freedom to move about the room, adding personal dynamics to the presentation.

Infrared and laser pointing devices are beginning to play a large part in the presentation arena (see Figure 13.4). It is possible for the presenter to mingle with the audience or roam around freely during the presentation. These remote control devices, when pointed at the projection screen, allow the user to control the function of the presentation from anywhere in the room. This action mocks the action of moving the mouse and pointer on the screen, freeing the presenter from having to be at the computer. Some hardware and software manufacturers offer

Figure 13.5
A notebook computer connected to a large screen monitor by connecting to a NTSC converter.

products that allow the user to make annotations or to electronically mark up the presentation. This feature provides electronic interactivity that rivals handwriting on acetate overlays on an overhead projector.

Monitor Mirroring

Another issue mentioned earlier in this chapter is monitor mirroring. Quite simply, this means that the contents of the computer screen are mirrored to the connected projection or display device. Typically, the presenter should face the audience while giving a presentation. When using a notebook or desktop system to control a presentation, the system monitor, or screen, should be facing the presenter, allowing a full view of the screen contents. This allows the presenter to make a quick reference to his presentation while maintaining eye contact with the audience.

The LCD panel, LCD projector, CRT projector, large screen monitor, or other presentation device, once connected to the computer, will project or display the presentation content exactly as it is displayed on the main screen. This display is intended for viewing by the audience while the computer display is for the presenter's eyes only.

Displaying Presentations on External Monitors

Connecting a notebook to an external computer monitor is routine. Connecting to a television is more innovative and a great way to effectively display your notebook-based presentation. However, connecting to a television set or monitor causes a different set of circumstances to arise. The resolution on a television is lower and requires a different signal interface than the computer sends to a computer monitor. Therefore a converter is required with a different transfer rate for images. These converters are priced starting at $200 and come with a variety of qualities and features. Consulting a user or qualified resource will be helpful when considering purchasing one of these units.

What About Videotape?

Even though notebook computers, overhead projectors, and LCD panels have been the norm in mobile presentations, there are other ways to display your productions while traveling. Digital technology in recent years has made it easier for the computer to interface with VCRs. With the connectivity between computer and video, it is now quite easy and inexpensive to copy your computer-based presentation onto video. The converter box mentioned previously will allow you to display your computer screen not only directly to a television, but also to a VCR. This will allow any information displayed on the computer screen to be captured onto videotape.

One advantage of using videotape is the fact that almost every company has a VCR and television in its conference room. Just pop the tape in and there you have it. If you are producing a video project for mass distribution, training, or product marketing, the same theory applies. Most households own a VCR.

If a videotape presentation is the medium of choice, and your plans include presentation at a remote site, investigation of on-site equipment must be considered. If the equipment is not available, then local rental or taking it with you are options. This all falls into the category of the importance of preplanning. As with all presentations stored on magnetic media, it is always a good idea to have a backup with you.

Considerations for Presentations On-the-Go

1. Prepare presentations with the presentation location in mind. If it looks good on your computer screen, will it look equally as good once projected through an LCD panel and an overhead projector?

2. When presenting at a different location, make sure that information about the room in which the presentation is to be given has been thoroughly investigated. Check for electrical supply, location and function of lighting controls, location of windows and the lighting control available at each, and acoustic details, etc.

3. Projected resolution issues are critical. Some information does not require exceptional resolution (charts, graphs, general information), while other information, such as specific training programs, require exceptional detail. Make sure the graphic resolution of your image, and the device that will project the information is capable of presenting resolutions that work.

4. When designing a presentation for use with an LCD panel, make sure the presentation, as well as the LCD panel, have the proper resolution for the job. Likewise,

make sure that the overhead projector is current enough to provide the proper projection brightness and clarity required to make the job work.

5. Look for equipment that supports "plug-and-play" ease of use. Newer equipment is easier to use in this respect. There are some areas that require technical assistance, and others that anyone can do. The best rule here is the rule of experience. The more familiar you are with the entire process, the easier success is to achieve.

6. The size of the screen is the determining factor in what size audience you can accommodate. You do not want a presentation to be too large for a small audience, or too small for a large audience. Talk to a presentation specialist for information on what size screen is appropriate for your target audience. Whatever you plan to present, it is important to ensure that it is presented as best as possible. After you have invested quality time and materials for your presentation, take the extra step to ensure that the audience sees it with the utmost quality.

Virtually everyone will have the need to communicate a message to some form of audience during the course of their career. Some possess the ability to do this without the aid of externals, while the rest of us require such support. As hardware devices offer more capabilities and we as users broaden our knowledge of how to use them, effective communication will take place naturally. With the newness of multimedia and all of the mystique surrounding it, there is no doubt that we will continually be bombarded with new products, processes, and resources. It will be our responsibility as a society dependent on technology, to pick up the tools that will support our need to communicate, and to use them to the fullest.

Glossary

AIFF—Audio Interchange File Format. A standard audio file format that is supported by applications on both Macintosh and Windows computer systems.

bit—A binary digit. The smallest unit of information that a computer can handle, represented by a single 0 or 1.

buffer—A part of the drive that reads information on the CD and stores it. This allows quick access to the information when you are ready to use it.

bug—An error in a program or a malfunction in a computer system.

bus—The wire or network of wires and circuits that carry signals from one part of a computer to another.

byte—A group of eight bits (representing, for example, a number or letter) that the computer operates on as a single unit.

CD-ROM—Compact Disk, Read-Only Memory. A data storage medium that utilizes laser optics to read or retrieve information. These disk store information in recessed "pits." The information on CD-ROMs is very secure and durable, due to the phyiscal structure of the disk and the plastic coating that protects the information. CD-ROM readers can also read audio CD formats.

CPU (central processing unit)—The main part of a computer. Contains internal memory, an arithmetic/logic unit, and control circuitry. Performs data-processing, timing, and controlling functions.

database—A collection of information organized for rapid search and retrieval.

data transfer rate—The speed associated with the rate that a CD-ROM drive reads data from the disk.

desktop case—The design of the computer housing. A desktop case takes up more space on the desk and usually allows for a monitor to be placed on top of it.

device driver—Software that tells the computer how to communicate with specific hardware devices. Some of these devices are: CD-ROM drives, printers, external speakers, and scanners.

disk drive—A device that rotates a magnetic storage disk that can record and read data.

downsampled sound—A sound originally recorded at a higher setting, then lowered, thus decreasing the size and quality of the original file.

DRAM—Dynamic Random Access Memory. Most graphic cards contain DRAM. It is cheaper than VRAM.

EDO RAM—Extended Data Out RAM is faster than traditional RAM. EDO RAM is recommended for graphic or data intensive applications, such as multimedia. EDO functions at 16 nanoseconds. Standard RAM functions at 70 nanoseconds

EIDE hard drive (Enhanced Integrated Drive Electronics)—The method in which the hard drive is connected to the CPU. Not only does it describe how it is connected, it describes how data is transmitted between the two.

expansion card(s)—Circuit boards, designed for a special purpose, that fit in one of the expansion card slots inside the computer. These cards are usually developed by companies that produce a specific peripheral device. The cards control how the device works. Some of the devices are: Scanners, monitors, sound, graphic accellerators, and audio/video input and output.

expansion slot—A socket inside the computer that will accept the variety of expansion cards.

file formats
> AIFF
> AVI
> BMT
> EPS
> EXPF
> FSSD
> GIF
> MIDI
> Paint
> PCX
> PhotoCD
> PICS
> PICT
> PICT2
> SND
> SFIL
> TIFF
> TGA
> RIFF

floppy disk—A thin flexible plastic disk that stores data in the form of magnetic patterns on its surface. Used primarily in microcomputers.

GUI (Graphical User Interface)—The physical appearance of what appears on your computer screen, usually refering to desktop metaphors, containing such items as trash cans, pull-down menus, icons of files, etc. The user can point and click on icons of folders, files, and applications.

hardware—The physical components of a computer system, such as the chips, disk drives, monitor, and other devices.

icon—A visual symbol of a program, document, or utility, that can be made up of almost any picture or graphic. Icons for application programs and their files usually resemble each other, allowing the user to easily recognize what type of file or application it is.

interface—The hardware and software that enable a user to interact with a computer (called a user interface) or that enable two computer systems to interact.

ISA (Industry Standard Architecture)—An earlier form of computer system architecture. Allows boards to be inserted into the computer on the expansion slots which are a part of the motherboard. Compared to the PSI Bus Architecture, ISA is much slower, and is not workable for video playback.

memory—A storage area in which a computer saves data and from which it retrieves data.

microcomputer—A class of small, general-purpose digital computers built around a microprocessor. Home, personal, desktop, and small business computers are all microcomputers.

microprocessor—A single chip containing all the components found in a computer's central processing unit.

MPC—Multimedia Personal Computer. These are usually IBM-compatible systems that offer built-in equipment, such as: CD-ROM players, speakers, microphones, and large disk drives, in order to play CD-based multimedia titles.

multimedia—The combining of two or more forms of media to effectively create a sequence of events that will communicate an idea in a audible and visual format. Multimedia components consist of animation, graphics, photography, sound, text, and video.

network—A system of computers, terminals, and databases connected by communications lines. Allows users of different types of computers to exchange data and to make use of special programs or very large computers. Scopes range from local-area networks (LANs) to international networks.

OLE—Object Linking and Embedding.

operating system—A linked series of programs that control, assist, and supervise all other programs on a computer system and that allow dissimilar hardware systems to work together.

PCI (peripheral component interconnection) bus architecture—The bus analogy refers to channels that are used to send data to different computer components and back. Bus architecture is a simple reference to the type of bus that your system uses. PCI is a newer technology that is found in IBM-compatible as well as Apple Macintosh systems. PCI Bus Architecture is one of the fastest processes to move information from one location to another.

pipeline burst cache—This cache is designed to take advantage of the PCI architecture. The term pipeline comes from the fact that the cache is connected directly to the PCI slot in the CPU. The term burst comes from the process of information and the retrieval of data is faster due to this improved cache system.

Publish and Subscribe—A feature, available in numerous applications, which allows imported files to be modified in their original state, and to be automatically updated, no matter where they are located. An "edition" file is created as a go-between, to continually update edited materials.

RAM (random-access memory)—A temporary computer memory system in which data can be stored and from which data can be quickly retrieved.

ROM (read-only memory)—A permanent computer memory system containing data and instructions that can be retrieved and used but never altered.

sampling rate—The process of converting analog sound into digital sound. The computer captures many samples from the original sound source and converts the information into digits that a computer can read.

SCSI (Small Computer System Interface)—A device on your computer that allows the connection to various periepheral devices such as CD-ROM drives, printers, or external disk storage.

SMPTE (Society of Motion Picture and Television Engineers)—SMPTE is also a name associated with a coding method used for videotape in the editing process. A SMPTE timecode has four formats:

1. 30 fps   (NTSC)

2. 25 fps   (PAL/SECAM)

3. 24 fps   (film)

4. 29.97 fps   (drop frame)

SMPTE Time Code—Society of Motion Picture and Television Engineers. The SMPTE time code provides an absolute address in hours, minutes, seconds, and frames for video.

sound card—A circuit board installed in a computer that adds sound capabilities to the system. Older systems often do not have sound capabilities. Most current systems are equipped to handle sound.

SoundEdit 16—Sound editing software that allows the user to record, edit, modify, play, and store sound files. SoundEdit supports 16-bit sound recording. SoundEdit 16 is manufactured by Macromedia.

tower case—A tower case refers to the design of a computer housing. This case design is vertical and takes up very little space on the desktop. These cases are also excellent for placing on the floor, totally away from the monitor and keyborad.

VRAM (Video Random Access Memory)—VRAM is more expensive than DRAM, but is faster and greatly improved the overall performance of a video card.

WAVE (.WAV)—A sound standard format for Windows sound files.

Index